# YOUR BEST FINANCIAL SELF

Edward C. Sanchez, RFC®

**VICTOR E.E.**

PUBLISHING

Victor E.E. Publishing, LLC
7061 W North Ave #353
Oak Park, IL 60302-1002

For information about special discounts for bulk purchases, please contact Victor E.E. Publishing at Contact@VictorEEPublishing.com

Library of Congress Cataloging-in-Publication Data:

Sanchez, Edward C., 1977–

Your best financial self / Edward C. Sanchez. — First edition.

pages cm

ISBN 979-8-9926686-2-9 (paperback)

1. Finance, Personal. 2. Financial literacy. 3. Budgeting. 4. Personal development. I. Title.

HG179.S265 2025

332.024—dc23

Library of Congress Control Number 2025938334

To Ivelisse: You bring color, music, laughter, and clarity to my world.

To Victor, Eiva, and Eli: You have given me greater purpose, and I hope these words guide you in becoming the best versions of yourselves.

# Table of Contents

# Prologue

## The Spark

When II was five years old, I remember riding in the backseat of my dad's 1982 Oldsmobile Toronado. It was just the two of us, driving to a credit union on the west side of Chicago. My mom and two sisters remained behind at our apartment. My parents had been arguing, and I could tell that my dad was upset. The whole drive to the store, I sat in the middle of the backseat, hoping his anger wouldn't shift onto me.

As we walked in, my dad almost appeared uncomfortable, as if he did not belong there. I didn't understand why he kept his eyes pointed down, his posture softened, and his energy almost apologetic. As I looked around at other people in the credit union, they seemed normal, smiling, and comfortable.

I didn't understand. If we were there to get some money from my dad's account, why was he uncomfortable? Why didn't he walk in with his shoulders pinned back, and head held high? This made me feel as if I should also feel intimidated or shy about walking into the credit union myself. With the tip of my nose pressed up against the edge of the Formica counter, I was barely tall enough to see the withdrawal and deposit slips in their slots. I remembered my dad filling out these forms on previous visits. He would fill out a form, we'd stand in line, he would talk with a person on the other side of the counter, and they would give my dad money.

This time, though, my dad wasn't withdrawing money from his account; he was there to take out a loan from his credit union. There was some financial emergency back home, and my dad needed money to fix the problem. I don't remember what the problem was. The primary issue was that my dad did not have the money to resolve it, so he needed to take out a loan. I asked my dad if he would have to pay it back, and he said he would pay it back on payday. This really confused me. I needed clarification on how my dad would borrow money today and then pay it back on payday, on top of all the other bills he typically had. I knew my parents regularly argued about not having enough money to cover the bills. My dad needed more money and would repeat the borrowing and payback process repeatedly. This was my childhood.

My dad was a serviceman for the Chicago Transit Authority, washing, repairing, and maintaining the city buses. My grandfather also worked for the CTA, but as a driver; he started driving buses in Toledo when he returned from his service in the army.

If it had a motor or an engine, my dad could take it apart, put it back together, and make it run better than new. My dad enjoyed his work but hated his job; in the seventies and eighties, racism was an ever-present reality of city jobs and departments. Even so, my dad also had the uncanny ability to flip people's moods. He could instantly defuse most heated arguments and have everyone laughing, preventing a fight or further escalation. My dad was funny, quick with a joke or a cool story. Everyone who got to know my dad liked him and wanted to hang out with him.

My dad has two sisters; he is the middle child of the three. After graduating high school, my dad attended trade school to learn air conditioning and refrigeration. He spoke English very well, having learned it in Puerto Rico. Despite his prodigious skills and trade school education, my dad struggled with money. He was never able to master it. My dad always had nice cars, but that was through his ingenuity, not his bank account.

My mother's side of the family was a little different. My grandmother had twenty pregnancies in total; four miscarriages, three of my mom's siblings did not survive past the age of two, and my mom was number twelve of sixteen. My mom grew up in Mexico with her thirteen surviving brothers and sisters. In her home, work was valued more than education. My mom did not attend school beyond the sixth grade. Even so, she learned English when she arrived in Chicago. She would eventually complete her G.E.D both here and in Mexico. My mom learned early on that she would get ahead by working her tail off, and nothing would substitute for hard work. As such, she was the better money manager by far. My mom looked for opportunities to invest in real estate and supplement the household income. But because my parents' financial personalities rarely aligned, they were never able to seize those opportunities.

My parents had so much to learn—their new American culture, their city, their jobs, each other, and this whole money thing—while raising three children. Despite facing foreclosure many times as a child, eating modestly, wearing hand-me-down clothes, and buying clothes on layaway, I had an incredible childhood.

My sisters and I always had a roof over our heads and never missed a meal, even if our extended family had to help us get groceries when my parents ran out of money. The money part was never figured out, not before they divorced. As a child, I did not understand how everyone around us seemed to have better lives. They drove better cars, had nicer furniture, and ate American meals without beans and rice. I became more perplexed when my dad took us to visit his coworkers and their families. I was blown away when I walked into one of his friends' garages and saw that he had a boat and a much nicer car than we did.

If this guy worked where my dad worked, why didn't we have nice stuff like this guy too? This was a mystery to me, and it ran through my brain day and night. Every day I saw examples of people living more comfortably than my family. It wasn't until high school that I began to understand that our financial struggles were not the result of a lack of earnings, but the mismanagement of them. With my parents' combined income, we should have been much better off and not living paycheck to paycheck.

Despite getting a glimpse into the root of our money problems in high school, I still didn't fully understand it until after college. At a very young age, I decided I would not live as an adult with a cloud of financial despair over my head or my house. I knew I would work hard, be successful, drive a nice car, have a beautiful family, and not be worried about money. I would not be bashful or timid about entering a bank to withdraw my money. I would be comfortable and confident. I would belong.

I began to understand that financial well-being wasn't about earning more money, but rather was about managing what you already had more effectively. However, it took me another twenty years to realize that better money management was actually step two. Step one involved shedding all layers of self-doubt and liberating oneself from the pressures of ego and keeping up with others who masked their own insecurities through spending and consumption.

### I Just Wanted to Be Rich

As a kid, I didn't know I wanted financial security; I only knew I wanted to be rich.

I didn't instinctively like school. But I knew that in order to be rich, I would need to be smart, which meant getting good grades. So, I set out to do just that. I focused on my classes and excelled in math, especially.

When I was nine, we moved from the Austin area of Chicago to Logan Square. It was still a very blue-collar area of the city. We now lived very close to two different grocery stores. From the age of ten until I was fifteen, I did our family grocery shopping every week. I would take our folding cart, the grocery list my mom put together, and $80 cash, down the steps of my front porch, through our chain-linked fence, and up the block to the main street.

I could tell you the change in price of green peppers, vegetable oil, a head of lettuce, a gallon of milk, a bag of rice, a box of cereal from one week to the other. I would read the weekly flyer, and I could pick out when there was a reasonable price on pork chops or ice cream. All the butchers knew me. They would lean over the counter to see the top of my head and tell me not to wait in line, but instead to walk around to the side of the deli counter and tell them what I needed. The butchers were always kind to me. But even at a young age, I hated feeling like I was getting special treatment. Despite the butcher's approval, I felt guilty cutting the line and worried the adults holding their deli tickets would get mad at me.

My mom put me in charge of saving the household money within our food budget. She'd say, "This is what I need you to buy, and this is all we have. You have to make it work." I loved the challenge; I had to find the best-priced items to stay within the budget. Initially, my biggest fear was overspending and telling the girl at the register that I would be leaving things. That was embarrassing and I dreaded that happening to me. It might have also been because many of the girls working the registers were in high school. While I wasn't in high school yet, I would have been horribly embarrassed if I had to leave an item because I didn't have enough money. I would see moms shopping with their kids, and they never looked embarrassed when they would have to leave an item or two at the register.

I eventually got so good at the weekly grocery that I could predict to the dollar the total cost before being rung up at the register. I was always looking for a bargain price.

The smashed rolls or the dented boxes were a favorite of mine. All the discount-priced goods were on the left-hand side of the first aisle as you walked in, just past the bread section. When I brought our groceries in under budget, I would throw in boxes of Jiffy muffin mix. Those boxes were twenty-five cents each, and I would buy four at a time because one batch would disappear from the kitchen counter before the second batch was out of the oven.

When my mom saw that I got the hang of this grocery challenge, she switched the game on me. She would make me buy groceries from both of our neighborhood stores. She would send me two lists, one for each store. I preferred buying everything from Tony's. This was the original Tony's before it burned down; they rebuilt and expanded into a successful chain of grocery stores in Chicago. Tony's Finer Foods had all the brands of food we saw on TV: Breyers ice cream, Manwich, Chef Boyardee ravioli, Ragú pasta sauce, Kraft macaroni, Entenmann's coffee cakes, and cereal like Rice Krispies, Frosted Flakes, and Cap'n Crunch.

However, my mom preferred me to shop at the Mexican grocery store, La Caridad. I didn't like going into La Caridad. It was smaller and not as well-lit. As soon as you walked in, you would be hit with the iron-blood smell wafting from the very back of the store, where the deli was. La Caridad had Mexican gelatins, cookies, and brands I had neither heard of nor wanted, but their prices were very competitive. I remember looking at the entire freezer section of ice cream and finding only one brand I recognized: Klondike ice cream bars. The rest of the ice cream was generic, typically in a plastic tub.

Despite my affinity for name-brand foods, we didn't have many in our house. Store-brand foods filled most of our refrigerator and pantry. The priority was to keep the shopping under budget. If I had, I would feel comfortable splurging on only one name brand item per week, like real Cinnamon Toast Crunch instead of Cinnamon Toasties.

My weekly trips to and from the grocery stores gave me time to think. I thought about my list and which items I would pick up, in which order. I preferred to go alone because my younger sister would just be a nuisance and pester me to buy her candy the whole time. My older sister was doing laundry and her household chores. As a result, I had a lot of time to think.

I thought about the most efficient route through the store to avoid double loops. I also kept my eyes peeled in my neighborhood. I scoured the sidewalk for lost change or money, or peered down the alley for hidden treasure. (I have no idea why I believed treasure would appear in an alley, unattended.) Still, I imagined I would find something of value discarded on my way to the store.

While surveilling the sidewalk for change, I counted the sidewalk squares to the store. Another time, I also counted all the black circles, which were dirty pieces of gum smushed into the sidewalk. I was always counting something: trees, cars, cans, anything that repeated itself in a pattern. Once I realized that there were enough cans to count, I started collecting cans. My dad regularly had scrap metal he would turn in for cash, so I started collecting cans to make money.

I would spot the cans on my way to the store, and after I returned home with the groceries, I would go back with a small bag to collect the cans. I remember feeling bad collecting cans in the alley when I saw a tattered person also collecting cans. I assumed he was probably homeless. I could see, he certainly needed the cans more than me. While I felt conflicted in those moments, it didn't stop me from earning money.

It was immensely satisfying to see the large black bags of smashed cans fill higher and higher on my back porch. When I would reach the point of stacking the bags on top of each other, my dad would take me to the recycler. These guys had a smelly, greasy-looking trailer set up in the parking lot of a nearby Venture, a local clothing-store chain. The guys would empty my bags into a fifty-five-gallon garbage can and then weigh it. Once they had it weighed, they would open their little register, take out my cash, and give me a handwritten receipt.

I thought this was amazing. I was getting paid dollars for picking up cans that others discarded as garbage. I remember wishing I was old enough to drive my cans to Michigan, where the recyclers paid even more per can.

I didn't understand how my older sister and younger sister watched me collect cans, turn that into cash, and never tried to do the same. I was pocketing real money, yet they seemed to have no interest. But it planted an idea in my brain: What is the secret to motivating people toward making money? These days, I can state definitively that all people want financial security—

even if much like myself at a young age they cannot articulate it clearly to themselves. They know they don't want to struggle.

## My Journey as a Teacher

Before we go any further, first I'd like to thank you for picking up this book. Please note the blank spaces below for the date and time. Write down the date and time you start reading this book.

Today's Date: _____     Time: _____

This marks the beginning of our journey together. We'll revisit the date and time later in this book. Let's get started.

I have been a teacher my entire life. My first student was my younger sister, Susy. When I was in the third grade, I excelled in math and reading. My mom designated me to help Susy, who was struggling with her reading in the first grade.

In those afternoons and evenings, I recall drawing upon every ounce of patience I could find. Susy didn't pick up reading quickly, which really tested my patience, but I never got mad at her. I was always so turned off by family members who were impatient and would fly off the handle at any minor event. I would think to myself, "They have such little self-control." I thought of myself in the same vein, believing I had little patience. As a result, I was constantly monitoring and trying to regulate my own reactions to events, in an effort to do better.

I never wanted to feel like I was impatient with my sister. I believe she taught me more than I taught her in those sessions. Susy had a slow start but came around quickly. I don't take any credit; I just think she needed a little more time.

I was a sophomore at Lane Tech on Chicago's north side when I got my first real job. I took two buses—the Western and the North Avenue—to get to my job. I was a busboy at an off-track betting (OTB) parlor. Like many of the other hires, I didn't really have any experience. All I knew was to keep myself busy. So, I cleared tables and ashtrays, brought out food, refilled cups and glasses with coffee and water like clockwork. As a result, patrons often gave me cash tips.

My hustle quickly moved me up the line. My managers moved me to better money-making shifts, when the crowds were larger.

After a year and a half at the OTB, the general manager asked if I would like to move from the restaurant to the mutuals line. This was where the mutual clerks punched the wager tickets. I was making $4.25 an hour plus tips as a busboy, and I jumped at the opportunity to make $12.10 an hour as a mutuals clerk. At the age of seventeen, I was the youngest clerk in the state of Illinois to punch tickets for Arlington, International Racetrack.

The mutuals line was a whirlwind of activity, and in many instances, patrons tried their best to "quick-change" or cheat us. As an OTB, we simulcasted races from all over the country:

Pimlico, Saratoga Springs, the Fairgrounds, Monmouth, Del Mar, Santa Anita, and elsewhere. It was important to be good, fast, and above all, accurate. As a result of the chaos, we would have a rush at the windows, and multiple clerks would close their windows down to do a box count.

A box count is when you key into your machine for a balance, and you count all the money in your wooden drawer to reconcile your balance. This was time-consuming, and it was an indicator that something might be off. In this role, you had to be quick on your feet and good with numbers. Box counts typically happened after a clerk sensed they might have been shortchanged, quick-changed, or if they themselves had made an error in giving back change.

At the end of the shift, we would close all the windows, and all the clerks did their box counts. We printed our sales slips, put our cash in a clear envelope, and walked it to the main window with the safe. This is when I would hear coworkers exclaim joyfully, "Hey, I've got an extra $20!" I did not think that was anything to celebrate. If you made it to the end of your shift unaware that your box was up $20, the inverse could have happened as well. You could have ended your shift with your box short, maybe by much more.

I had my own system. I never lost eye contact with my bettor. I instantly repeated the bet back to them in verbatim, more clearly and phonetically than it had been shared with me, as I simultaneously punched in the bet. An exacta, perfecta, trifecta, partial wheel, or box, it all quickly added up. I would punch in the bet with precision and pause for a split second, staring at my bettor. I would pause for a validation or confirmation that I read the bet back correctly. Once confirmed, I would strike the enter key.

On many occasions, I had to slow a bettor down and remind them, "That bet's going to be $64 or $128, is that the one you want?" Their mouths would agree hurriedly; their bulging eyes would tell me differently. I knew instantly this bet was going to get pared down by a couple of horses. All of this was happening with three other bettors behind them, trying to shout their bets in too.

I didn't experience any surprises in my box at the end of my shifts. I knew to the dollar what was in my box and, as a result, I didn't need to shut down multiple times a shift for a box count. It also helped that I was so young; I didn't have any interest or desire in gambling myself. Clerks weren't allowed to bet while working, but that didn't mean it wasn't happening.

Again, my manager, Jack, saw my efficiency was helping him and I was rewarded with the task of training new hires on a regular basis. This was wild because I was a trainee, a few months back. Everyone else on that mutuals line was in college, out of college, had kids in college, or even grandchildren. Looking back, I am fortunate that the revolving group of adults in that department were kind to me and looked out for me. I may not have felt like I needed looking out for back then, but I was just a kid, and I definitely worked with a great group of people.

At the University of Illinois, I stumbled into a student resource leadership position at a dean's office. I think Dean Michael Jeffries saw how lost I was and knew instinctively that I wasn't going to ask for help on my own. His office offered me a job as a student resource leader so I would learn about and use the resources of the Urbana-Champaign campus, that I otherwise would be too naive to explore. That was a gift. There I was, teaching incoming students about the many resources the dean's office and campus had to offer.

As a child, I yearned for safety and security. My young brain interpreted the legal field as the surest way to protect myself and those around me. Today, I finally understand where the ambition to become a lawyer came from. So, after college, I started working at a law firm. First at one bankruptcy firm, then another. I spent six years at the second law firm, averaging over sixty hours a week. I wrote a training manual, which was implemented firm-wide in our offices across the country. I wrote the training manual because I was training so many new attorneys and clerical staff. I could not answer all their questions while simultaneously training the newest hires and keeping up my personal work production. I wrote the manual to replicate myself. I would train the newest associate or clerk for three days, and before I would hand them off to the next department, I would give them the training guide. I would say, "Read this; don't come to ask me any follow-up questions until you've read this cover to cover." Once again, I was teaching.

I left that law firm to start my own business. I co-founded a credit counseling firm to teach others how to manage their household finances to increase their success and create financial security. In the process of my entrepreneurship, I faced an opportunity to guest speak at my son's seventh grade investing class at his school. Due to budget cutbacks, the school lost its investments teacher. Within a few weeks, I went from guest speaking to teaching once a week. I started with just the seventh and eighth grades. I pivoted the material from the investing game to financial literacy. I curated a curriculum from resources I found online, and from my own work in credit counseling. I expanded the class to include the 6th grade. That one day of guest speaking evolved into twelve years of teaching financial literacy as an elective in my kids' school. My students and I had many successes, and multiple Money Smart Kid Champions and ambassadors to financial literacy in Chicago. The added time with the students and the benefit of being close to my children in the school led to coaching track and field alongside my wife. Teaching and coaching have been truly rewarding in my life. Young minds understand with precision the logical steps of sound financial management and the relationships of market movements. What they don't have are the lived experiences and perspectives of life's challenges and baggage, which can contradict the adoption of logical financial decisions.

I am not an attorney, I am a Registered Financial Consultant and as of this writing, more than 470,000 students have registered to take my financial education courses online. I didn't set out to be a teacher and I never envisioned myself as one, but I haven't been able to get away from having a life filled with teaching and coaching opportunities. My thirst for learning and passion for sharing my knowledge with others is rooted in my own personal survival. I do not doubt that every experience I have had in my life has been leading up to this moment.

Although I discovered that the mechanical steps to achieving financial security are not counterintuitive and do not defy logic, I was left with one heavy nagging question that would absorb my attention and drive the rest of my career.

*Why don't more people have financial security?*

I've studied consumer behavior, spending patterns, inclinations, financial tools, marketing, government oversight, regulations, financial products, and services. I have spent my lifetime trying to figure out the answer to this question. Even so, I believe there is a three-part solution to this question.

Firstly, we have to peel back the layers of self-doubt: both the ones the world puts on us, as well as the layers we put on ourselves.

Secondly, we have to understand the landscape—the financial chessboard, if you will—and recognize the traps, pitfalls, enticements, and distractions. We need to recognize that this gameboard is not designed to let either you or me win. Additionally, understand what you bring to the table. Not you the individual; you the collective member of our society and generational development. As you will read in the coming chapters, we are hard-wired for safety, survival, and comfort. These traits complicate our decision-making process, even as we face straightforward, yes-or-no problems.

Thirdly, we have to learn the mechanical steps needed to reclaim control of our finances and charge toward building true financial security. And yet, we can't do this without acknowledging and addressing the first and second parts of this three-part answer. Only when we face our self-doubt and take a clear-eyed view of the finance game, can we finally move toward a lasting impact.

Your lived experiences, your gender, race, culture, zip code, your parents, siblings, peers, and the whole ball of wax have shaped the lens through which you see the world and yourself in it. My goal is to help you discover your lens and even adjust your prescription, so that you can not only navigate safely, but chart forward with the clarity and confidence that'll unlock your light. That light which the world so desperately needs and deserves.

.

# PART 1

# PSYCHOLOGY

# Chapter 1

## The Psychology Behind Financial Decisions

### Your Perception Is Your Reality

In our current climate, our country is more divided than ever. It is challenging to shift others from their reality. Too often, we interpret our feelings as facts. Two people can witness the same events side by side but come away with completely different impressions.

It's crucial to interpret situations accurately; neither worse nor better than they are, but as they truly are. The better you interpret, perceive, and recall events, the more successful you'll be in navigating situations where others are clouded by emotions or biases. You might have a cousin or coworker whom you love but can't understand their thought process. This is often due to their inability to perceive reality without the influence of emotions or personal biases.

## Operating Independently from Your Ego

Recognize the distinction between your true self and your ego. Self-actualization means pursuing what you truly desire, not what your ego dictates. Think of a time when you fought for something you didn't actually want. It was your ego seeking validation, or in fear of being proven wrong. Prioritize your peace by being open to change and open to new information.

A trap many fall into is unconscious consumerism. If it doesn't serve your purpose or well-being, don't indulge in it. Understand your spending patterns and reasons behind them.

Observe how you live and the actions you take. Recognize the self-inflicted suffering your choices might cause. As Eckhart Tolle says, "I try to find myself in things, but never make it."[1] Often, we're not truly seeking products, but rather, identity enhancers. Accumulating products keeps us in this loop of chasing, working, achieving, spending, and yet, never truly arriving. You cannot find your true purpose, your passion, and your meaning on this planet, if you are merely surviving. You cannot shift from surviving to thriving without first kicking the ego out of the driver's seat.

The ego truly wants us alone on an island. The ego pushes us away from others, having us believe we are separate and not connected. The ego also pushes us away from the present moment. Being in the moment is being present with our truest selves.

In my experience, the ego tends to relate to the present moment (ourselves) in one of two ways:

1. As an enemy.

2. As an obstacle.

Treating the present moment as an enemy arises when you resent your present circumstances or regret past actions. This mindset leads to a cycle of blaming and accusing, forgetting that external reality mirrors our internal state. Ask yourself: Is the present an obstacle? Am I making it an enemy? Am I spending, buying, or accumulating to pacify this feeling of discomfort in the present moment?[1]

When you see the present merely as an obstacle, or a stepping stone to a future goal, you're never truly living in the moment. You perceive life as a series of problems to solve, always delaying happiness and fulfillment. This loop of postponing joy is endless, because the present moment is all we truly have. Work to quiet your mind, acknowledge your feelings, recognize them, and allow yourself to be present without judging yourself or others.

## Observe Your Energy

My own vibrational energy varies. I can recognize when my vibrational energy is lower than usual because I stress more as

---

[1]   Tolle, Eckhart. *A New Earth: Awakening to Your Life's Purpose.* New York: Penguin Books, 2005.

I focus more on myself. My worries become more prominent, heavier, and ever present. I'm more easily offended by the driver in front of me, I am more inclined to get bothered or upset by things being out of place in my home. All this stems from my ego pulling my vibrational energy level down by making me feel more important and less appreciated.

When my vibrational energy level is higher, I am in the same space, experiencing the same life events. Except my problems are not problems but opportunities to learn, grow, become more innovative, and adapt to changes for the better. I empathize with the driver in front of me, who must be stressed or lack adequate information to reach their destination. "Go on ahead," I think; they must be in a greater hurry than I am.

I don't have feelings of unappreciation or lack of support. When my vibrational energy is where I practice it to be, I am more at peace with my surroundings, who I am, and what I have. I am in complete appreciation of the moment. My focus is redirected from myself as an individual to myself as a part of my family, my business team, and my community. This is a perpetual exercise, as the ego constantly works to bring me back to "me" mode.

Remind yourself to appreciate what you have. Recognize your current resources and tools and realize you can achieve more with them. Don't let your ego hinder your growth. Without seeking external changes, you possess the power to shape your present and future.

Eckhart Tolle said, "There is no substitute for finding true purpose."[2] While prosperity might offer relative freedom, it can't provide a life filled with meaning. Your inner purpose is to be present and awakened. Waiting for a future event before truly living—be it retirement, a raise, or any other milestone—is a flawed approach. The blessings you need are already within you. Cherish the present and find passion, fulfillment, and gratitude in every moment. Being aware of your vibrational energy will help you align with the goals that serve your peace and not your ego.

## First- and Second-Order Rewards

I learned about the concept of first- and second-order rewards from Ray Dalio. He articulates this reality of life better than anyone I have seen. He says it's almost as if nature sorts us by throwing us trick choices. Those choices have two types of consequences: first-order and second-order. Life then penalizes those who make their decisions based on the first-order consequences alone. For example, eating food that tastes really good, such as a cinnamon roll (first-order consequence), can most generally be bad for your long-term health (second-order consequence). Conversely, eating food that is healthy for you in the long term, like broccoli (second-order consequence), doesn't taste as good (first-order consequence).

---

[2] Tolle, Eckhart. *A New Earth: Awakening to Your Life's Purpose.* New York: Penguin Books, 2005.

This is incredibly challenging because there are two dragons to slay here. The first is to avoid the temptation of that ooey-gooey cinnamon roll, and the second is to overcome the pain, boredom, or monotony of a physical workout. Those who can consistently slay these two dragons will experience overall more success in their lives. The goal is to achieve moderation in our consumption to assist and not hinder a regular exercise routine.

The neat reality is that we are creatures of habit. Once we can consistently delay that instant gratification and push through that workout, our bodies and our mind will crave more of the same.

Working out in the first-order consequence can be painful and boring. In the second-order consequence, you are healthier overall, your body learns to crave exercise, and it is no longer boring.

Everything in life is hard. Being broke is really hard. Every day, you will find the most straightforward tasks to be exponentially harder because of a lack of money. The reality is that creating true wealth and financial security is hard, too. Not having your health, not being able to be active, and not doing the things you want to do with your family is hard. Getting in a run or a workout when you don't want to is also hard. Here's the win, you get to choose which hard you want.

The true rewards are increased vitality, clarity of mind, and the freedom to live life on your terms. These only come when we navigate past those first-order temptations.

This book is a guide to help you bypass the first-order choices and better align with the second-order choices.

> *Limiting Financial Belief:* ***Money is private; I don't want to discuss money with family or with my kids.*** – How inclined is this person to advocate effectively for proper compensation at work or pass down strong financial principles to their kids? Lack of comfort with money is often handed down from those we love. Discovering your financial personality will help you break this cycle.

## The Six Financial Personalities

There is a big name in the financial guru space who narrows down all people into either nerds or free spirits when it comes to money. The nerds are unforgiving, and the free spirits are emotional and lack "brains" or reason. I don't believe this categorization comes close to understanding what drives the financial decision-making processes.

The way you think about money and debt affects your ability to achieve financial success. Many people carry negative associations with money from their youth into adulthood. They may believe that people who earn tremendous sums of money are greedy, those who spend significant sums of money are materialistic, and those who save a lot are scrooges. Although our beliefs may not always be apparent to us, they significantly affect our consumer behavior.

Whether you realize it or not, you possess a financial personality, as we all do. These personalities form early in life and root themselves in all your financial decisions. Understanding how you think about and deal with money helps you overcome bad habits and establish new good habits.

In my work, I've identified six primary personalities. Financial personalities extend beyond the simple categorization of spenders and savers. If that were the case, the savers could balance out the spenders. It's much more nuanced than that. Understand that your personality, tendencies, reflexes, and fallbacks reflect a substantial part of your personal development. Without awareness, you cannot adjust, correct, or improve. Your financial personality developed very early in life and has been reinforced by layers and years of experiences, both good and bad. The victory lies in recognizing your financial personality and improving upon it.

Today, I'm going to help you identify your financial personality. As I share these financial personality types, one or two may describe how you feel about money.

**The Pessimist**

The Pessimist believes that living in debt is a way of life. They are content with their debt and gave up trying to live debt-free long ago. A common trait of Pessimists is to continue to consume and spend despite their financial despair because they have already resigned themselves to a life of debt. Without judgment, I can observe that the Pessimist has been burned in the past and this is their process for creating a semblance of security.

The Pessimist did not start out this way, but after what feels like a never-ending barrage of financial emergencies, mishaps, accidents, unfair fees, and more, the Pessimist has grown tired of fighting. Fatigued, the Pessimist opts to end their fight with debt, and they surrender to it. This does not bring real security but does bring calm to a weary warrior.

## The Spender

The Spender can rarely be dissuaded from purchasing something. They have transformed shopping into a sport. For the Spender, it's not even about the kill but the hunt. As a result, Spenders buy stuff they don't even need. As a compulsive shopper, the Spender rarely has savings and often finds themselves in a financial bind. The Spender has an aspirational quality to their ways, in that they know how to live in the moment. Living in the moment is special and important, but it certainly requires balance.

It's important to note, the Spender is not born a Spender. Now more than ever, we've become acutely aware of our inclination to chase that dopamine hit that comes from something new. The Spender is not intentionally trying to accumulate things. The Spender is trying to fill a void and despite all they buy, the void never fills up. I find that many consumers get pulled into the Spender lane as a result of overexposure to ads, social media, and frictionless ways designed to separate us from our money.

## The Procrastinator

The Procrastinator knows they should save a minimum of 10% of their income for retirement but postpone saving for a time when they'll earn more money. On the surface, the Procrastinator believes that not only will nothing catastrophic impact them personally, but also that everything will work out even better than naturally expected. The main problem with delaying saving for retirement is that, most often, when a person earns more money, they find a way to spend more money. Ultimately, Procrastinators will reach retirement age with little or no savings.

At the root of procrastination is fear. While not having a nest-egg for retirement is scary, getting wiped out in the stock market may feel even scarier. Like the Pessimist, and the Spender, the Procrastinator is navigating in a way that provides them with the greater sense of security.

## The Easily Overwhelmed

The Easily Overwhelmed have resigned themselves to being victims, having decided that managing their money and controlling their spending is too much to handle. The Easily Overwhelmed often end up transforming into the Pessimist. At some point, the Easily Overwhelmed felt rescued in their despair or felt entirely abandoned in their despair. The rescue felt so good that that learned helplessness was more comfortable than charting toward risk and independence. If it was abandonment instead of a rescue, then the Easily Overwhelmed has found comfort in their despair. The Easily Overwhelmed finds comfort in what they know and discomfort in the uncharted, even if the uncharted offers a better quality of life.

This book will teach you how to minimize your risk, while increasing your probability for success. You'll learn how managing your income and expenses are simple tasks and can be mastered.

## The Giver

While being a Giver is a beautiful thing, it can be hazardous. The Giver never thinks of themselves first and gives until nothing is left. To their detriment, the Giver will lend you money and even co-sign for you. The Giver finds greater joy in helping someone else than in building their own financial security.

The Giver may feel unworthy and moves to protect themselves by denying themselves and giving to others first. Nothing can be taken away, if they don't have anything to take. This is survival. The Giver insulates themselves from any hope of comfort or luxury, avoiding a potential letdown or disappointment and finding peace in giving joy to others. I personally know a Giver. My older sister is the biggest Giver I know. Having fallen on the sword many times with our parents in order to protect her younger siblings could be what has attributed to her being a Giver in her adult life.

## The Super Saver

The Super Saver has a superpower. They are often the easiest to spot. Being known for frugality and unwillingness to splurge can quickly create a reputation. The Super Saver enjoys greater financial security and is more likely to have peace of mind. They possess the discipline necessary to put money away and avoid temptations.

The Super Saver is perhaps the most guarded of all the personalities. It is likely, the Super Saver learned early in life that the world is not going to protect them; they will have to protect themselves. They feel this so strongly that they will pass on simple pleasures, and certainly luxuries, for the security blanket that is savings.

The one potential downside to being a Super Saver is not enjoying the benefits of years of discipline. This would be the kryptonite to their superpower. The Super Saver must learn to enjoy their hard work and sacrifice. You can't take it with you. In retirement, it is essential to recognize the security blanket has done its job and it too can retire from a long career.

I want you to understand, I need you to understand, the implications of your financial decisions: why you make them, why you persist in certain behaviors, and whether these decisions are bringing you closer to or pushing you further from your goal of financial security.

Have you identified which personality you relate to the most? It's ok to exhibit aspects of several of these personalities. However, being overwhelmingly one personality type is not ideal.

If your dominant financial personality is not serving you for good, it is because it is driven by fear and motivated by a feeling of scarcity. You can work your way out of an unhealthy personality by starting with gratitude. Recognizing your financial personality is the initial step toward achieving a balanced mixture of these personalities. Understanding these personalities can redirect your future actions and decisions toward the goals of your true self, not your reactive self.

## Your Financial Personality Is Your Compass

Consider the compass. Have you ever used one? I believe they're invaluable tools. A compass, with its circular dial and magnetized needle, always points to magnetic north, thereby reliably indicating which direction is north based on your orientation. Your financial personality acts as your magnetic north, consistently pulling you in a particular direction.

When I meet with a couple to conduct a financial analysis, I ask about their goals. It's often heartening to see that their financial goals, more often than not, align quite well. However, their financial personalities can be dramatically different. Imagine you and your spouse, your life partner, are in a rowboat. You have only each other, and you've discussed and agreed upon your destination. You're both rowing as hard as you can, yet you find yourselves being pulled in different directions.

Can you begin to perceive how being unaware of your financial personality can impact your life? It's crucial to understand and be aware of your spouse's financial personality, and equally vital for your spouse to recognize and comprehend yours. That's why, when both are presented with the same financial event, you might see an opportunity while your spouse perceives risk, or vice versa.

Consider others in your home: your children or perhaps your parents. What are their financial personalities? If they wield purchasing power in your home and have access to your money, it's essential to comprehend their financial personalities. Can you think of a few relatives who agonize over making large purchase decisions, taking them six months to decide which refrigerator to buy? While other relatives don't suffer from purchasing paralysis because every time you see them, they have something shiny and new?

Understanding your spouse's perspective won't lead to instant agreement, but it will facilitate better communication and mutual understanding. This will enable you to work as a team, like on that rowboat, to achieve your financial goals together. Financial trouble is often cited as one of the leading causes of divorce in the United States. How can you row effectively if you're being pulled in different directions? Many people simply try to row harder, hoping that this will resolve their money problems. I'm here to show you that rowing harder won't save you, but rowing together will. Even with my robust, efficient, and proven strategies, you won't implement them if they don't align with your psychology. That's why I begin with your psychology and dedicate so much time to this topic.

First, we must change our thoughts, to change our behaviors, in order to achieve the results we desire. Which personality is your dominant personality? To take the free Financial Personality test today, scan the QR code below or visit my website at: www.sixfp.com

## Align With Source, and the World Will Conspire to Help You

You're surrounded by teachers and synchronistic events, yet often you can't see them. Step out of your own way and let these teachers reveal themselves. I believe in God as the creator of the universe and all things within it. If you believe in Allah, Brahma, Vishnu, or any other divine spirit, consider the term "source" as a reference to your creator. For me, God is that source.

We are born into this world to serve others through our unique skills, insights, personalities, and creativity. This is an alignment with "source." For instance, as a professional athlete, you serve by offering entertainment, exhilaration, and motivation. As an actor, you provide an escape, allowing audiences to momentarily step into different worlds.

The service provided by professions like researchers, doctors, nurses, teachers, and lawyers are easier to see. However, even if you work in a call center or at Dunkin Donuts, you're serving. You help bridge the gap for someone, whether it's by answering their questions or providing them with a caffeine boost to tackle their day.

When you prioritize your own needs and fail to see your connection to others, you might perceive scarcity in the world. You'll likely encounter others who share this self-focused view, making your journey even more challenging. However, when you align with a higher purpose with source, to serve others, the universe will conspire to help you accelerate and achieve your mission. You might find that opportunities and connections arise in the most unexpected places, from a scholarship nomination to a career-changing offer based on your dedication in a seemingly unrelated job, via a seemingly unrelated interaction.

These serendipitous events occur daily. Your vibrational energy can attract connectors who will assist you without seeking personal gain. Their reward is the joy of making meaningful connections. Conversely, when you're self-centered, many of the people you encounter might only offer help if there's something in it for them, hindering your progress.

> *Limiting Financial Belief:* **I will focus on the short term and the present and work hard. Then, I'll be able to catch up later.** The reality is that tomorrow never comes.

# Chapter 2

## Common Fallacies

### The Someday Trap

Dan Ariely is a professor of Psychology and Behavioral Economics at Duke University and author of several best-selling books. Dan has discussed the concept of irrational optimism in various contexts, often highlighting how our biases and cognitive processes lead us to be overly optimistic in ways that defy logical reasoning. Despite logically understanding an irrefutable fact, such as two in ten people will suffer a serious injury before they die, we believe that in a room of one thousand people, we or the people we know could never be affected. Additionally, we are surprised, if not shocked, when this event occurs to someone we know. Flying further in the face of this denial is an irrational expectation that we are the exception. This is the reason why millions of lottery tickets are sold every year. Despite this reality, according to the National Weather Services, getting struck by lightning is about a one-in-a-million probability. Separately, the chance of winning the Powerball jackpot is one in 292 million.

If you were to poll people who have purchased lottery tickets, if they feel they are 292 times more likely to be struck by lightning than winning, they would not agree.

It is far better to live a life with some irrational optimism than none, but it is more important to be aware of it and how it impacts our ability to accurately measure risk and opportunity. Saving for tomorrow starts today, not tomorrow. The future you will thank you.

## I Have Lost Everything

### Only the Ego Can Claim: I Have Lost Everything

There is no such thing as "I have lost everything," for there is nothing to lose, only to experience temporarily. If you lost your job, house, career, or relationship, you would still have yourself; if you love yourself, that would be enough. If your father disapproves of you, that is his bag to carry, not yours. You could never earn his approval because he lacks the love within to love himself and, in turn, lacks the capacity to love you.

Identifying with what we have and what we do is identifying with ego. Ego will tell you, you are separate from others. You are better, you have more, or you have less and you are inferior. Let go of ego and all that you could lose vanishes, because there is nothing to lose. The material and the egocentric become distant as your peace becomes your new comfort zone.

When you have nothing to lose, you have nothing to fear.

## Who Fears Failure More, You or Your Ego?

The notion of ownership is just that—a notion. It's a mental construct that, when faced with the inevitability of death, dissolves into insignificance.

Eckhart Tolle eloquently states that while people "were looking throughout their lives for a more complete sense of self, what they were really looking for, their Being, had actually always already been there, but had been largely obscured by their identification with things."[3] This attachment, this identification with the tangible, blinds us to our true essence. It's as if our mantra becomes, "I have, therefore I am." The more we possess, the more validated we feel. Yet this sense of self is fragile, always dependent on external validation, always comparing, always wanting.

This constant yearning, this insatiable "need for more," is the ego's trap. It's a voice that whispers, "You're not enough yet." The fleeting satisfaction of acquisition is quickly replaced by the itch of desire, leading to feelings of unease, restlessness, and anxiety. It's crucial to remember: whatever we resist, persists. Don't wage a war against debt; instead, embrace the concept of abundance. Don't rail against illness; embark on a journey toward wellness.

---

[3] Tolle, Eckhart. *A New Earth* (New York: Penguin Books, 2006).

Eckhart Tolle introduced the concept of the "pain-body" in his book.[4] Tolle describes the "pain-body" as a semiautonomous entity within us, thriving on negative energy. It feeds on our emotional turmoil, our dramas, and our negativity. It's addicted to unhappiness. This addiction to negativity, this lower vibrational energy, manifests in impulsive spending, splurges, and the endless cycle of consumerism. While momentarily soothing, these actions sabotage our future selves and our higher goals.

To truly ascend, we must recognize that everything, from the tangible to the intangible, is energy vibrating at different frequencies. Thoughts, though unseen, are simply energy at a higher frequency. Negative thoughts vibrate at lower frequencies, while positive ones resonate higher.

Generations pass down this "pain-body," this reservoir of negative energy. Children, absorbing the emotional states of their parents, often become the next carriers.

To break free, we must shift our perspective. Instead of carrying disdain for creditors, embrace financial security through self-value, vigilance, and financial moves that serve you genuinely. Seek higher vibrational energies, as true wealth is beyond the material.

---

[4]  Tolle, Eckhart. *The Power of Now: A Guide to Spiritual Enlightenment* (London, England: Hodder Paperback, 2001).

## The Balance of Gain and Loss

Identify the ego in the instinct to avoid pain. By removing the ego, you'll discover it's easier to pursue gains than to avoid losses.

We've all experienced pain in life. Loss aversion is based on the notion that people are more driven to avoid losses than to seek gains. Our brains naturally recall our losses more vividly than our gains. Because these losses are more prominent in our minds, we are instinctively driven to steer clear of them. This instinct often holds us back. There might be opportunities to achieve a personal milestone or acquire a new skill, but the potential for loss or failure looms large. This brings us again to the concept of first- and second-order consequences. If you can set aside your ego's fear of potential rejection or failure, you open yourself up to the second-order benefits of growth, success, and personal validation.

If security is your top priority, understand that you will face minimal risk, but you'll also see limited personal or financial growth.

When presented with an opportunity to gain something, remember your financial personality and remember your ego's inclination. If the potential of a perceived loss looms larger than the potential for growth, pause, take a breath, and evaluate what is driving your gut in that moment.

## Good Earners Are Good Managers

I want you to stop believing making more money is the primary way out of your financial troubles. Making money is part of the solution, but for most, it's just a small fraction of the solution.

A few summers back, my family and I were invited to a boat adventure off the coast of Massachusetts. The boat accommodated eight to ten people and was equipped with a navigation system, including a display screen and tide data. The plan was to take this boat out and to navigate around some of the small islands off the coast.

My knowledge of boating is extremely limited, but bear with me. As we prepared to "set sail," we had to untie the boat from the dock, reverse it and then navigate out of the marina. From the get-go, there were multiple opportunities for things to go awry. We needed to be mindful of the tide—I learned this was the "water level." We needed to steer clear of any sandbars and maneuver within the designated buoys. The navigation system had to be operational, the radio functional, and the life vests at hand. Everything needed to be in alignment.

As we made our way, we had to be aware of the current, the tide, the wind, and other vessels. When it was time to anchor near the beach, we also needed to consider the time of day, how long we'd stay, where the tide would be when we were ready to leave, as well as how it would affect our route back through the sandbars and islands.

Now, imagine that every mistake—not leading to total devastation but minor errors—resulted in a "tax." Each time we failed to anticipate, react, and operate in an optimal and efficient manner, we would incur a "tax" penalty. For novices like myself, these "tax" events would have accumulated quickly and become incredibly costly. If I wished to continue boating, would you suggest I aim to earn more money to cover these "taxes"/expenses?

Or is it possible for me to operate the boat more intelligently and efficiently in the future, thereby avoiding many of these taxable events? Indeed, having more money means I could afford more mistakes, but that doesn't equate to efficiency nor enjoyment. Moreover, if my family is with me, I'm not teaching them how to operate efficiently either—simply how to cover my mistakes with money.

If I were to fully grasp the grandeur and power of the ocean, along with the intricacies of the tide, the waves, and the wind, I could improve my skills. Further, if I studied my vessel's operations, mechanical systems, and emergency procedures—and engaged in extensive practice—I could significantly reduce the frequency and severity of those errors and their costs. If I evolved into an experienced mariner, would earning more money be necessary to continue boating and managing these tax events? More money would be nice, but not necessary.

I chose boating as an analogy because it's a realm far removed from my area of expertise, and it perfectly illustrates how quickly situations can escalate from ok to devastating. This parallels how we manage our finances. Regrettably, access to financial education is lacking in our schools, leaving many to navigate these waters without a basic understanding of what to expect.

Many people are good earners and, as a result, they don't really feel those "taxable events." Despite their inefficiencies, they acquire larger boats and venture into more dangerous waters, mistaking deep pockets for navigational skill. Meanwhile, the vast majority are adrift, at the mercy of the current (the market), hoping to avoid financial disasters they cannot afford. Overwhelmed by helplessness and despair, they focus almost exclusively on the one aspect they believe they can control: working harder and longer to earn more money.

As guests on this boat, my family and I had the privilege of taking in this incredible and memorable experience. Meanwhile, my head was on a swivel. I was watching the captain navigate, assess, plan, maneuver, and communicate back to land. I remember thinking how much I would have messed up or how many things I would have gotten wrong if I had been in charge, simply because of my lack of knowledge and lack of experience. Had I been captain and had I been "taxed" for every miscalculation, our beautiful day out on the water would have been entirely different.

If I had to repeat that boat outing day after day, as life requires us to navigate day after day, I would have accumulated a hefty tax balance. I would put my family entirely in financial peril before learning all that I needed to prevent future "tax" events, much less succeed. For some, that financial peril takes years to recover from, and those early mistakes really weigh down not only their trajectory toward financial security but their psyche and perception of self-worth as well.

Our life experiences, our exposure, our upbringing, our education, our environments, and our backgrounds all play a role in how we navigate in life. Don't fault yourself if you're not where you want to be today, because we do what we can with the tools that we have. I honor you for seeking better tools.

# PART 2

# THE
# LANDSCAPE
## AND HOW
## WE NAVIGATE IT

# Chapter 3

## Actual Truths

### The System Is Not Set up for Us to Win

If you have not yet achieved the level of financial security or success you desire, it's not your fault. The landscape you navigate is riddled with tricks and traps. Additionally, we all harbor a set of contradictory inclinations and survival instincts that often work against us. Every debt solution offered by lenders is merely another debt product. Lenders don't earn more when we manage our finances efficiently; in fact, their profits increase when we falter. It's not in their interest to provide genuine education in this area; instead, they offer more products.

Allow me to draw a parallel between physical health and financial health. Our financial health status significantly influences our ability to apply prudent, necessary measures. Let's look at these stages: triage, recovery, improvement, and optimization. In an emergency room, triage is about survival. Recovery requires professional guidance and patience. Then there's improving health, a stage where many of us believe we are. Finally, there is optimal health, where maximizing our physical and mental peace becomes part of our daily routines. Professional and expert assistance is required at every stage to ensure success.

If you've had the misfortune of being driven to an emergency room in an ambulance, you can relate that in that stage, you would not be receptive to recommendations for vitamins and supplements. No matter how sound those recommendations may have been, they did not apply to your needs at that moment. The same applies to finance.

We understand the value and benefits of saving and investing for the future. However, when we are in a state of financial triage in our daily lives, these indisputable truths about saving and investing don't resonate; they become irrelevant.

I meet clients at every level of the financial spectrum: from my junior-high finance students, who have no obligations, to young professionals considering homeownership, to parents with kids in high school, who are struggling with debt and worried about college expenses. Lastly, I meet seniors, many of whom look back, wishing they had prepared more effectively for this stage in their lives.

Whether you're in financial triage (survival), recovery, improvement, or optimal health, your status isn't necessarily linked to your age or life phase. Too many people progress through life stages, from childhood to retirement, without ever leaving survival mode.

Only after you observe and acknowledge you are in survival mode can you work to exit and exit it as soon as possible. Most people remain stuck in survival mode despite earning more money—even substantial sums of it. This is because escaping survival mode isn't about the amount you earn; it's about how you *manage* what you earn.

Reading books about money, attending seminars, and seeking education are part of the journey, but these resources won't resonate or be applicable until you're out of mental survival mode. Trying to leap from triage to optimal health is not probable, yet most believe they can. Investing while in survival mode will lead many to chase after big wins and fall for promises that are too good to be true, ensuring that you remain in survival mode—or worse, fall further behind. I want you to understand this, so you recognize that your current situation isn't your fault.

Breaking out of your current situation requires understanding both the external factors you face and what you're capable of achieving when you begin your journey from within. Armed with this understanding, you're better prepared to undertake your financial transformation and take ownership of your progress. Utilize the fundamentals in this book to move beyond your current situation, both mentally and financially. Removing financial insecurity will fast-track your progression.

## Banks Are Smarter than You and Me

I can tell you with absolute certainty that no credit card company will offer you a product that benefits you before it benefits them. The lending industry has access to billions of dollars in resources. They employ people with graduate degrees in economics and finance who understand how to design products like credit cards and loans that generate interest and huge profits. Banks have no incentive to be philanthropic in their business model. Instead, their objective is to continue to generate greater profits year after year. They achieve this by devising creative and tempting strategies to part us from our money. Some of the most popular tactics include zero-interest credit card transfers, deferred payments into the distant future, and no interest for the initial twelve months. Credit card companies bank on you, becoming distracted and losing focus.

Here is how a 0% interest credit card transfer breaks down. When you initiate a balance transfer, a transfer fee is levied, typically 3% or 4%. So, right from the start, the lender profits from you. With a zero percent interest credit card, the minimum payment is set so low that your account balance grows even when you make a payment. This phenomenon is called *reverse amortization*. Your monthly payment is so minimal that you're only covering the interest on the credit card, barely making a dent in the principal. When you're comparing the previous minimum payment on a 19% or 29% credit card to the new 0% interest credit card payment, you'll likely find a significantly reduced payment. That reduced monthly payment will give you the illusion of a win. However, a lower monthly payment and a soon-to-expire 0% interest offer are merely the magician's cloak and wand concealing the reverse amortization that makes your balance go up, month after month. There are credit cards that promise no interest for the first twelve months, but these cards still accrue interest during that period. Once the twelve months elapse, if you haven't paid off the balance, the lender will retroactively apply all the accrued interest from that "no interest until..." time frame.

## Planned and Perceived Obsolescence

### *Planned*

Manufacturers of goods (such as office furniture, home furniture, computers, phones, etc.) have realized that if they manufacture their goods to last a lifetime, they can sell their goods only once. Manufacturers plan and design their goods for two purposes:

1. To last long enough for the consumer to fall in love with the product/brand,

2. To fall apart where repair is not an option, only replacement.

Once both are accomplished, the manufacturer has a client for life.

We see this with cars. So many parts are made of plastic. Sure, the manufacturer offers a sixty-thousand-mile warranty, but they've already designed their parts to last just long enough to surpass the usage of the warranty. These same car parts could be made and cast from aluminum, which is not an expensive metal. But, if they were made of aluminum, the part would last essentially forever and negate the need for repair or service with the car dealership.

There is no better example of planned obsolescence than the smartphone. If you have an iPhone or Android, you know that after twelve months, your phone starts lagging and running slower, almost like clockwork. Batteries could have a longer shelf life, but that would work against the business model of a quicker and more frequent upgrade by the consumer. Your battery no longer holds the charge it did when new. All this makes for a very unpleasant experience, which prompts us to upgrade our phones.

### Perceived

From UGG boots to Stanley water mugs, trends move our culture. Other trends include switching from dark wood floors to light ones, wood kitchen cabinets to white, and black appliances to stainless steel (or hidden altogether). Trends come and go, making consumer goods, furniture, and clothing appear less valuable simply because they do not represent the latest and greatest. Once you understand this manipulation, you will be more inclined to look for items that are less trendy but can stand well over time.

Once again, cell phone owners can attest to the intentional change in design from rounded edges to flat edges on the phone and the same on iPads. These changes are designed to be large enough so the naked eye can detect if you are an early adopter, an in-time consumer, or a Luddite. Even the green-versus-blue-bubble debate in your group chat is intentionally designed to differentiate and show status.

Being aware of planned and perceived obsolescence alone is not enough to shield our desires to upgrade our goods, but it helps make informed purchase decisions rather than emotional ones.

## Surfers Don't Get Mad at Waves

Life is both beautiful and brutal. It does not care what you like or prefer. Get good at adapting. Getting stuck on the world not going your way will only ensure that you continue to struggle. Every American success story has its share of pain, loss, and struggle. Success does not come without struggle. Most success stems precisely from the struggles that people encounter and overcome. Get good at overcoming obstacles.

I recently watched a fascinating documentary on surfers chasing one-hundred-foot waves. Facing retirement from a career of surfing, Garrett McNamara accepted an invitation to visit the waves in Nazaré, Portugal, in person. What followed would be a career-changing discovery and journey into chasing one-hundred-foot waves.

It was remarkable how Garrett and his team were being thrashed around, pulled under, and thrown into consecutive spin cycles. Despite these oceanic beatdowns, the surfers never got mad at the waves. They fully understood that these beatdowns were all a part of the process. Garrett pioneered the use of a coordinated team, including Jet Skis, helicopters, photographers, videographers, radios, and high-point lookouts, all working in unison to tow the surfers to the optimal wave opportunities and simultaneously yank the surfers from imminent death under those crashing waves. The surfers never rode to shore talking about how the wave was supposed to go "this way" or "that way." Instead, they knew they could not predict exactly what a wave would do or even if and when it would arrive. What they could do was prepare, prepare, and prepare some more so that when a wave appeared, they were ready to take massive action.

Life is a series of waves. There are glorious waves that you will ride, waves that you will miss and waves that will all but knock you out. The question is: will you get mad at the waves? Will you get mad at life, or will you be able to look inside and do a self-assessment? *How well did I handle that wave? What could I have done differently to improve my chances of success? What will I do when the next wave arrives?* People get mad all the time. I hear them say, "That stock was supposed to do this." They'll back-test, apply filters, and look for patterns to explain and forecast what a stock should do. Waves are going to come, and if you're not ready, they are going to knock you on your ass. If you get mad at the wave, the trading platform, or whatever is outside of you, you will continue to fail to grow. You must look within to find how you can better prepare and how you can improve. Be like Garrett and those surfers: prepare, prepare, prepare, and don't get mad at the waves.

## When We Make More Money, We Spend More Money

I often hear, "I'm in debt. I need to make more money. I just need a raise. If my boss wasn't so horrible. I need a better job. If only I had my dream job..." All these thoughts position the solution outside of oneself, pointing the finger outward rather than inward. Looking outside of yourself or beyond the present moment is not the solution. And having more money doesn't inherently make you a better saver or a more efficient money manager. If you were reckless with finances when you had little, winning the lottery would likely just make you a more extravagant spender, at least for a while.

Merely earning more money won't protect you if the economy crashes; not even an enormous income can guarantee that. However, strong financial discipline and responsibility can safeguard you from economic downturns, regardless of your income level. Many professionals—like bankers, doctors, and accountants—face financial struggles, even leaving their families in debt upon their deaths. We've seen countless entertainers and athletes declare bankruptcy. Their downfalls weren't due to a lack of money but a lack of financial knowledge and discipline. These individuals didn't suffer from job losses or economic shifts but rather from mismanaging their wealth. It takes discipline to break free from the tendency to spend more when you earn more. Remember, it's not how much you make, but how much you keep and grow, that will create the financial security you deserve.

The average American, however, can face job losses, economic downturns, and even natural disasters. They can also suffer from poor financial management and living beyond their means. It's crucial to be aware of these risks. Imagine if your job suddenly disappeared or if an illness or injury prevented you from working. How long could you maintain your financial stability? Now, imagine the same scenario but with a safety net of four months' expenses worth of savings. Wouldn't your job search be less stressful? Wouldn't you feel more secure knowing you could support your family for a while? Achieving this is more feasible than you might think.

Picture a third scenario: you lose your job, but your home is fully paid off, and you have zero debt. While this might seem like an unattainable dream, it's not. The perception of it being impossible is a narrative pushed by the banking and consumer industry. In reality, the average American is fewer than eight years away from complete financial freedom. When you learn how to manage your earnings effectively, you can reach this freedom more easily than you think.

The strategies in this book will show you how to pay down your mortgage, car, student loans, credit cards, and miscellaneous debt, build savings, and manage your lifestyle without getting a second job or working overtime in just eight years or less.

That may sound like a long time, but ask yourself how many eight-year cycles you have lived through still carrying the same amount of debt (if not more).

## "Save 10% First" Doesn't Make Sense to Me

I hear financial experts online and on the radio. They advise you to save 10% first, but they don't explain how. My clients seek me out because they want answers; they're in search of solutions. They don't approach me because they've got everything figured out. The principle of saving 10% seems out of reach for them. So, when someone advises them to save 10% off the top, it just doesn't resonate.

My clients describe their financial situations to me: for every dollar they bring in this month, they're paying one debt because that creditor demands it. Next month, they might skip that payment to address another bill. They wonder how they're supposed to meet all their obligations if they're only working with ninety cents on the dollar. The reality is, they can't. It feels like they're being told to magically do more with less. But remember, when you change the way you look at things, the things you look at change.

Through my courses, I offer my clients a systematic, comprehensive approach that combines multiple strategies. I've crafted a method for managing your budget that allows you to take total control of every dollar you earn and every dollar that enters your household. Once you implement this system, you'll discover that you can manage your expenses, reduce your debt, and even have more than 10% to set aside for your retirement.

Why limit your savings to just 10%? That doesn't seem logical to me. I suggest that you take complete control of your budget, refine your lifestyle, understand your spending habits, and save as much as you can. You must do this because you deserve it.

## The Decline of Vacation Time Amidst Rising Work Stress

In 2023, various studies highlighted a concerning trend: Americans and Canadians are opting for fewer vacation hours, citing work-related stress as the primary culprit.[5] Some workers express guilt about leaving their already understaffed teams behind, while others feel chained to their constant obligations and demands.[6]

Although the overall nature of our work has shifted from labor-intensive tasks to more administrative roles, the mental load of

---

[5] "Despite Financial Stress, many Americans are too worried about job stability to take PTO" https://www.bankrate.com/credit-cards/news/pto-and-financial-stress/.

[6] "How Americans View Their Jobs" https://www.pewresearch.org/social-trends/2023/03/30/how-americans-view-their-jobs/.

juggling responsibilities, deadlines, and client demands remains heavy. In our pursuit to manage this load, we turn to business coaches, consultants, and conventions, hoping for solutions to enhance productivity and streamline operations.

Imagine, for a moment, facing the same professional responsibilities tomorrow as today, but without the financial burdens of mortgages, medical debt, car payments, or children's tuition. How would you approach work differently, knowing these financial responsibilities were no more? My bet is that you'd feel considerably lighter and more focused. You'd engage more actively with colleagues, empathize with their stresses, and lead more effectively. It is financial stress and insecurity, more than any deadline or demanding client, that amplifies our stress and eats into our deserved leisure time.

If you've ever returned from a vacation stressed, take a pause and assess what was really behind that stress.

You want to move away from your compounded financial obligations and move toward fewer obligations and greater financial security. Ironically, financial security will provide you with more mental and emotional relief than multiple vacations could.

## Not Everyone Wants to Be a Millionaire

While many voice the desire to become millionaires, the path to such wealth—marked by relentless work, continuous learning, immense sacrifice, and personal and societal risks—isn't for everyone, often, when faced with the reality of what it entails, many opt to remain in their comfort zones. If you worked an average of forty hours per week, from the age of eighteen to sixty-five, and never earned more than $17 an hour, you would have earned more than $1.6 million dollars. Now, that's not how much you take home, much less keep, but you would earn over one million dollars. As a part of Generation X, I know the collective aspiration was to become a millionaire and to "buy Mom a big house." That's what media and culture pushed as the ultimate idea of success. In real life, however, this is not what most adults aspire to, even though it is an admirable goal. More and more frequently, the sentiment I hear is: *I don't want to be rich; I just don't want to struggle anymore.* That right there is the underlying desire we all have, the universal aspiration that binds us all: the quest for financial security.

Despite not having the desire to hustle, fight, sacrifice, grind, and more for the sake of earning millions, many find themselves doing the exact same, just to break even, only to be knocked down again by another financial emergency. This is exhausting. According to a 2022 Pew Research study, 29%, one-third of Americans, are below middle-class earning levels.[7]

---

[7] *"How the American Middle Class Has Changed in the Past Five Decades,"* Pew Research Center, last modified April 20, 2022, https://www.pewresearch.org/short-reads/2022/04/20/how-the-american-middle-class-has-changed-in-the-past-five-decades/.

You can get off this crazy, hustle, grind treadmill much easier and much sooner. The idea is to first stop digging. No more new debt. Secondly, pay down your debt while building a financial umbrella for emergencies. Lastly, convert your financial umbrella into a financial parachute for your retirement. All these details will follow in Part III.

## Shame Shrinks Everything in You

If you are feeling shame about the level of debt you have or the lack of money in your life, you are identifying with that debt. I will remind you; you are not what you have, and you certainly are not less if you are lacking. Shame shrinks everything in you. Shame is the opposite of self-actualization, where every part of you expands and enables you to help others.

When you feel self-actualized, you have higher energy levels, you do whatever it takes to achieve your goals. Nothing can stop you, and the impossible becomes reality. By contrast, when shame has you in its grasp, you beat yourself up, your energy drops and it becomes even harder to overcome. Everything seems impossible. Then you come up with negative beliefs about yourself, and what you're feeling in the moment becomes your reality.

If you think you're screwed up, you're going to color yourself that way. Can you break free? Yes, of course you can. There is no value in beating yourself up. Take responsibility for your actions without harsh self-judgment. Your ego has to let go of shame. However, positive self-talk also needs action to really work. Wishing alone won't grant you a financial windfall. I will show you that although the system is not set up for you or me to win, we can make it work for us.

One of the keys to affluence is breaking the vise grip of limiting financial beliefs. I believe you can—you *will*—achieve financial security in a healthy, productive, helpful, and ethical way.

## The Illusion of Earning Our Way Out

Stop chasing money. In the short term, earning more money can mask many problems. We repeatedly witness the unfortunate reality of money disappearing when managed by someone lacking financial skills. We can't earn our way out of poor financial decisions.

Only financial mastery will solve your money problems. It is a very common mistake to operate backward. We make poor financial decisions and then hope to earn more to compensate for those errors. We create the problem first and then hope to fix it in the future. Instead of preparing first and then making more sound decisions, you must first take control of your mindset in order to take control of your money. The exciting part is that once you master your finances, you can achieve so much more with the money you already earn.

You can't negate bad financial decisions or habits simply by earning more. As people's income increases, their spending often does too. Income will fluctuate; it doesn't always rise steadily. Don't be short-sighted. When you're doing well financially, be cautious and always prepare for unforeseen setbacks. Income interruptions, whether from job loss, injury, illness, or the loss of a loved one, can occur when you least expect it.

## Wealth: Birthright, Fate, or Self-Made?

In my work, I have found three distinct categories that define our financial beginnings. First, there's inherited wealth. Some are born into families so affluent that even youthful financial blunders won't lead to ruin. These families often have wealth managers and a family office guiding their fortunes, ensuring a cushion against common mistakes.

The second group wins what I call the "genetic and environmental lottery." These individuals, due to a unique blend of DNA and circumstance, are destined for wealth, irrespective of their initial financial conditions. Consider Benjamin Graham and Warren Buffett. Neither was born into affluence; Graham even faced financial hardships. Yet, their innate talents, paired with the times they lived in, set them on paths to immense wealth.

The third and largest group lacks generational wealth and lacks a familial financial blueprint. Their financial education, often riddled with errors, comes from well-meaning but misinformed sources. They're inadvertently taught to create small leaks in their financial boats, steadily sinking into financial drama. This group works the hardest, for they are not just working to get ahead; they are also working to compensate for the leaks in their boats. This flies in the face of the theories that poor people are poor because they're just lazy or don't work hard.

However, hope isn't lost for this third group. With the right mindset shift and guidance, they can rewrite their financial narratives. Often, these individuals are lured into believing their issues stem from cash flow, seeing consolidation as a solution. But the real problem isn't cash flow; it's internal mismanagement. Blaming external factors like jobs or markets is futile, as these are beyond one's control. Owning the problem is the first step to owning the solution.

If sweat equity, hard labor, and grinding long hours ensured wealth and financial security, we would see an instant flip between the ultrarich and the poor. Wealth and security are not created by hard work alone, but it is definitely required in the beginning. From our tax system to investing, security is granted to people who create savings, acquire assets, and invest, not to those who only know how to work.

My work and research have centered around identifying that pivotal moment, the switch, when one transitions from a mindset of scarcity to one of abundance. This book is my aim at a replicable model to guide my readers toward financial independence and security.

# Chapter 4

## Consequences of Ego-Driven Financial Decisions

### The Twin Traps of Income Creep and Lifestyle Creep

Recall your college days. How often did you survive on peanut butter and jelly sandwiches or ramen noodles? As a cash-strapped student or a young adult venturing out on your own, stretching every dollar was the norm. In those early years, with limited earnings, it was unsurprising to have scant savings.

Fast-forward to today, where you might be earning double or even quintuple what you did back then. Yet, I've met countless clients whose earnings have soared, but their savings remain stagnant. With increased income often comes increased expenditure. It is absolutely vital to resist this allure. When you start earning more, seize the immediate chance to prioritize saving and investing. Eventually, when your savings grant you security and your investments flourish, you can then consider elevating your lifestyle. An elevated lifestyle with no security is not elevated at all.

## Unexpected Blessings: Recognizing Gifts without Bows

Sometimes, the universe nudges you in the right direction, especially when you're hesitant. From my perspective, this guiding hand is God's. I've witnessed countless tales of individuals trapped in jobs they loathe, gripped by fear of the unknown, only to have that very job yanked away unexpectedly. The immediate reaction is often despair, with the pressing questions "Why now? Why me?"

I've seen these moments of adversity transform into opportunities. People who clung to the safety of familiar jobs have ventured into careers they once only dreamed of, thinking them unattainable. Similarly, God sometimes intervenes in relationships. Many recognize the toxicity of a certain relationship but lack the courage to end it. And then, a glaring sign appears, making it impossible to ignore any longer.

It's essential to see challenges as opportunities rather than problems. God's delays are not God's denials. If your prayers seem unanswered, perhaps it's not because you're unworthy but simply unprepared. As a younger man, I yearned for riches. Yet, had I attained it prematurely, I might have squandered it or failed to use it for greater community good.

God's blessings don't always come gift-wrapped. Often, they manifest as harsh wake-up calls. But within these challenges lie profound lessons. They teach resilience, insight, and personal growth.

Consider the thought: not all gifts come adorned with bows. For many, a seemingly adverse event, like a layoff, is a hidden blessing, a catalyst for change they'd never have initiated themselves. So, how will you leverage such gifts? Will you uncover the embedded lessons or let them pass unnoticed?

Strive to be indispensable in any role you undertake. Whether it's time, money, or credit, learn to harness these resources wisely. As Ray Dalio, the acclaimed investor, wisely puts it, "Mistakes are inevitable." But they're also invaluable learning opportunities. Embrace them, for they're simply signs that you're progressing.

Dalio further states that energy, like money on a balance sheet, cannot be destroyed—only transformed. Whether it's equity, debt, or income, it's all about allocation and reconfiguration.

Continuous growth is a journey of consistent learning and improvement. And while perfection might be elusive, every mistake brings you a step closer to your goals. So, cherish those setbacks and challenges because they are the most valuable gifts you will receive.

## Don't Wish for Overnight Success

Sometimes you're just not ready. If God had given me everything I wanted when I asked for it, I would have pissed it away or ruined it. At the age of twenty-four, I left a good-paying job. I was making $74,000 a year, and I thought I had arrived. I thought I knew what I needed to know to teach others. I thought this was only the beginning and my earnings would only go up from there. I left that secure job, went out on my own, and started my own business. I was not ready. For the next two years, my business would generate negative revenue, and I would burn through my savings, cash out my 401(k), and create an additional $200,000 in debt. I was all in. I did not know enough to avoid what I felt at the time was unavoidable. There were many signs of the looming real estate crash. Looking back, it should not have surprised so many of us.

Ultimately, I was too passive; I mismanaged time and deadlines, leading my real estate project to hit the market in the spring of 2007. Here's the reality: had I finished a year prior and on schedule, I would have netted a solid gain on my investment, and I would have reinvested my gains into an even bigger real estate venture, just in time for the real estate crash of 2008. Instead, I was wiped out like so many, and my losses, despite monumental, were capped. That gift did not come with a bow on it. It was a gift nonetheless, and it anchored how I would manage my businesses going forward.

I was now in a position to experience financial failure and struggles, not as a child but as an adult. It would take me and my business partner fifteen years to pay off the debt created in our first business venture, all while starting a new business from scratch. I needed those hard lived experiences, to learn and be able to curate and develop the financial education courses that would resonate, relate, and speak to the thousands of students who take my courses every month.

## Money That Comes Fast, Often Leaves Faster

Fast money gains do not make us good stewards of money. Think of the gold rush, the tulip mania, the dot-com boom, the real estate crash, Bitcoin, Bored Apes, and NFTs. The stories of people speculating, wishing, hoping, praying, and getting wiped out vastly outweigh the number of success stories. We see this on TV every night. A game show contestant has just won $30,000 and they can take it home or they can risk it all for a chance at $75,000. The contestant is genuinely torn between her options, but the audience is not torn. They're shouting in unison for her to pass on the guaranteed money for a chance at a bigger win.

If this same woman was approached on a typical Wednesday morning in her office, with no stage, no lights, and no audience, and offered $30,000, do you think she would be just as flippant with that money? She would not because she would feel from her soul to her shoes how hard and how long she has to work to earn that much money. The reality is that game show money is not offered at work, much less on a Wednesday morning.

Success is not linear. Seize opportunities, lock in your gains, and create safety nets for yourself, understanding that you are increasing your probability of success when you're faced with the next one-hundred-foot wave.

## Your Need for Acceptance Is Making You Invisible

Judging yourself because you don't have the same shoes, clothes, home décor, cars, or lifestyle will put you in an endless cycle of trying to mirror your perception of someone else's life instead of experiencing the exceptional version of your own. The perpetual need of the ego to be liked by others pushes us to seek acceptance by mirroring what others do, say, and how they spend their money. Seek acceptance from within and celebrate your individuality. Your strengths, points of view, passions, and interests are what make you unique. Embracing your uniqueness and strengths will help liberate others around you who are shackled by their own insecurities. When you accept and love yourself first, the world will embrace you quicker.

## You and the Joneses

Just like when you were a child riding in your parent's car at night, you looked up at the sky and convinced yourself that the moon was following you. You understand now that the moon was not following you. Today, every financial guru out there takes turns blaming the Joneses, blaming them for your desire to keep up with the Joneses.

I want you to think back and reflect with me. Much like the moon following your car, wasn't it odd that there were Joneses at your elementary school, then at your high school; you saw them again when your kids were in preschool, and now that your kids are in high school, they're back again? The common denominator between you and the Joneses is you because they keep changing, but we keep calling them the Joneses.

I don't subscribe to the notion that we are collectively trying to keep up with our own "Joneses." I believe that the Joneses represent something different to all of us. When we meet them, we discover something which makes us feel uncomfortable about ourselves. So, it's not the keeping-up part that drives our rampant consumption; it's the inner child who is still longing to feel safe. As adults with spending power, we jump and spend to heal, pacify, and protect our insecurities, which we project onto this lovely and unsuspecting family, the Joneses.

As uncomfortable as it may feel, I want you to avoid pointing your finger at the Joneses. Yes, they have a lot of really nice new stuff. Point your attention inward and reflect on how being around the Joneses makes you feel or makes your ego feel.

Only then can we break this perceived cycle of one-upping each other.

## The Dual Dance of Fear and Greed

Robert Kiyosaki insightfully analyzes the intricate dance between our emotions of fear and greed—and their influence on our financial behaviors. Many of us begin our careers employed by others, chasing a consistent paycheck. This quest for financial security is where fear takes the reins. In the process, we often sideline our passions, neglect precious moments with loved ones, and sacrifice personal interests. Essentially, we trade our irreplaceable time for money.

Then, with the money we earn, we fulfill our basic needs and then our desires, too. Yes, a reliable vehicle might be essential for commuting, but an $87,000 car? That's a luxury, not a necessity. It's our lack of understanding of what drives our consumption that keeps us tethered to this relentless cycle of working and spending. The fear of losing these possessions, coupled with the insecurity of living without the status they represent, keeps many from leaving unfulfilling jobs.

This cycle, once established, is formidable. Not everyone inherits a business or starts with a silver spoon in their mouth; most begin their adult lives working for someone else, and that's perfectly fine. The challenge is to balance our aspirations with reality. Earn your paycheck, but let passion guide your choices. Ward off the temptations to self-soothe via consumerism, and focus on the essentials and living within your means. A solid foundation of savings and assets can offer the security to extinguish any fears. When you are not weighed down by financial anxieties, you can access the space to explore, invest, and even venture into the high-risk world of entrepreneurship.

## We Create the Chains That Bind Us

We are born with limitless potential and then we meet life. We become our own biggest critics, and in the name of preserving our ego and our self-esteem, we hold back. We embrace safety and shy away from putting ourselves out there for others to see trying. Life or people around us will tell us we're not good enough, not fast enough, not strong enough, and we decide, be it on the playground or in the classroom, to agree or disagree. It can be even harder to disagree when we echo the same words to ourselves. This is your opportunity to recognize that anything you have achieved up to this point in your life is because you chose not to listen to negative feedback. You chose to push beyond. It's time to keep pushing.

## The Pitfall of Overindulging Through Our Children

A recurring trend I've observed is parents forgoing personal indulgences to provide their children with experiences they never had. But beneath this surface of the "self-denial" lies a more profound, emotional act of living vicariously through their children. While it's heartwarming to watch your child enjoy something you missed out on, caution is essential. Every desire doesn't need fulfillment, and every whim doesn't warrant indulgence. Children showered with every imaginable luxury often grow into adults with unrealistic expectations. Recall the entitled kids from "Willy Wonka and the Chocolate Factory." Their unchecked desires didn't win them any favors.

Consider the earlier times when acquiring a dream sports car was a symbol of decades of hard work and savings. Older men splurging on these cars were often labeled as undergoing a 'mid-life crisis.' Today, easy credit access has shifted this timeline. Young adults, fresh into their careers, can now own these same sports cars well before the receding hairline, dad bod, and years of building up savings and credit. Young adults aspire for homes grander than their parents and seek more lavish and more frequent vacations. Such mindsets, unfortunately, may stem from childhoods where desires were instantly gratified, often swiped on a credit card or acquired through debt. With credit, you can have it all; you can have it now. Moderation is key to grounding urges of instant gratification, both for our well-being and that of our children.

## React or Anticipate: The Choice Is Yours

Losers react, and leaders anticipate. Prepare, and you will have more options when confronted with a challenge or an opportunity. Think of the last time you had to buy last-minute airline tickets. Did you have a lot of options and were they in the perfect price range? No, you had very few options, and those options were more expensive than you wished for. When you anticipate and prepare, you have more options, and your eyes are open to spot opportunities. Preparing increases your likelihood of success. Reacting ensures you have fewer options.

## Don't Worry about Looking Good

Focus on being the person you want to be. Do you want to win, or do you want to be right? To win is to have someone agree with you and to be in harmony with you and your idea. You get to choose the restaurant; your project will be next, or your suggestion is accepted. To be right is to feed your ego by proving someone else wrong. There is no harmony when you let your ego lead. You may win the point or the argument, but you've lost harmony and peace. If you practice leading with your ego, your ego will only want more winning at the cost of others and more separation from those around you. When you practice keeping your own harmony and peace, you not only allow others around you to be at peace, but you also attract higher vibrational energy, which will accelerate your journey to success.

## Ask Empowering Questions

Learn to ask the right questions. You've asked your brain mid-conversation before: "What's the name of that actor in that one movie with the thing and that other thing?" Your brain could not have come up with the answer during your conversation, but your brain did not stop searching. Two days later, when you are caught up in something completely different, your brain says BAM! I found it! It's Bruce Willis, and he plays the detective in the movie with that other guy. You gave your brain a search command, and your subconscious mind continued to work until it could close that inquiry, even if your conscious thoughts had already moved on. You want to harness this unbelievable power to your benefit. Ask better and more empowering questions. Ask questions that move you toward your dreams. How can I travel to Europe next year? How can I get a job working in my dream industry? These are the questions your brain will work on and continue to work on until you find the answers you need.

The inverse is also true. Never ask, "Why me?" If you ask this question, your mind will remove you from the solution equation and will look for only external factors to point to your woes. You and I understand that any solution, joy, and success you experience in this life will start with you. So, you cannot remove yourself from the solution by asking, why me? A better question to ask is, what am I supposed to learn from this? It's not easy at first, but with practice, your magnificent brain will come up with some brilliant answers. Those answers will add to your arsenal of knowledge and experience that will better prepare you to face future obstacles and challenges. Master the art of asking yourself empowering questions.

## We Are Finishers

Remember those visits to your grandmother's house as a child? The ritual always began with a warm, cheek-pinching greeting.

Almost immediately, she'd ask if you were hungry. And within moments, you'd find yourself perched on a chair that felt too big, your feet dangling, waiting with anticipation at her kitchen table covered with that unmistakable clear plastic cover.

Grandma would uncover lids, steam rising from boiling pots, and she'd move spoons and ladles like the conductor of a symphony orchestra.

When she finally set that plate before you, it was a veritable mountain of deliciousness. You'd glance up, eyes wide, insisting there was no way you could eat all that. She'd simply smile and say, "Eat what you can, dear. I'll handle the rest."

Two powerful forces then came into play. One is an undeniable appreciation for your grandma's culinary expertise. And two, that profound urge to make her proud. So, armed with a fork and knife, you'd embark on a culinary journey, navigating through every morsel. Before you knew it, that plate was empty, much to your astonishment and your grandmother's sheer joy.

What drove you to conquer that mountain of food? It's rooted deep within our psyche. We are inherently finishers, wired to seek closure. When we embark on a task, we're innately driven to see it through to the end. While completing tasks brings a sense of accomplishment, it's equally vital to approach life with an open mind and discernment. Marketers and car salesmen specifically understand very well that once we've started the car shopping process, we're hardwired to finish this task. They understand we want to metaphorically close that open loop; as such, they don't hesitate to put unfavorable terms in front of us and watch us as we close ourselves. They understand the forces within us that tip the scale in their favor.

Finishing what we start is important. Finishing out a long, grueling basketball season with very few wins is more about being there for your teammates than stacking up wins. Honoring your commitments is not only commendable but essential. The distinction is to be aware of this hardwiring in your brain when you enter into a journey like buying that car. In that instance, your finish-at-all-cost mentality could override your savvy bullshit detector. Although achievement is the goal and feels great, it isn't the actual foundation of financial security. We're trying to move away from a win/lose mindset.

# Chapter 5

## Goals: Take Ownership of Your Journey

### Transformation, Not Achievement, Is the Win

You can't chase what you already possess! If you chase abundance, you'll perpetually be in pursuit. Seeking abundance externally is an endless endeavor. You already possess the capability to control your finances and choices; there's no need to chase. Recognizing it already within you is what will free you from continuous searching.

Save yourself from decades of searching for something that was within you all along. You simply labeled it differently and, consequently, couldn't recognize that it was already in your possession.

Don't beat yourself up every day because you haven't established a million-dollar company. Don't berate yourself daily if you haven't reached your target weight or can't fit into those clothes. Celebrate yourself for being the only person working diligently toward your goal every day. You're the person who is actively taking steps. You are the achiever; you're just at the beginning of your journey. You are victorious from the day you decided and began that journey, not just when you hit a milestone. You are the one who rises after a setback. Applaud yourself for your consistent efforts and for striving for your betterment.

You might think, "This approach won't work. If I'm lenient with myself every day I don't meet my goal, how will I progress?" I believe many of us have unhealthy relationships with our goals. Instead of serving us as motivation, they just act as the unreached benchmark we use to beat ourselves up on a daily basis.

You can track your growth. If you fail, learn, and then improve rapidly, your evolution will soar. If you're not doing it effectively, your development will decline. Measure, monitor, measure again, and adjust.

Relish the journey, the hard work, the sacrifices, and the attention to detail. Appreciate your growing skills and how you've streamlined your processes. You have learned and implemented all of these. Frankly, you're kind of a badass and kind of a big deal.

James Clear points out that success is not just about reaching a specific goal; it's about personal transformation. Rather than focusing solely on the end goal, emphasize your personal growth. Celebrate every step forward, no matter how small.

## Self-Compassion: Breathe. You'll Be Okay

For years, I didn't recognize that my insecurities drove my judgment of others. It's easy to think you judge others because of their appearance or because they seem to seek praise or attention. However, I urge you to look closer.

For instance, when I criticized—silently or out loud—what someone wore or how they spoke, I now recognize that I was actually judging myself. Perhaps not in that exact moment, but because I constantly criticized my own appearance and actions, I unknowingly projected those judgments onto those around me. I believed I was witty and discerning. In reality, I had a fragile ego. I was so concerned with how others saw me that I constantly judged myself. It wasn't until I truly learned to love myself that I noticed a cessation in my judgment of others.

I came to understand that someone else's fashion choices were none of my concern. My opinion was irrelevant. By not wasting thought or energy on such superficial matters, I could better appreciate the inherent good in people and connect with them more genuinely. All those years of mental self-chatter about inconsequential and irrelevant matters were really just a shield against my own self-judgment.

This pattern is evident in online comment threads. Someone lashes out, and a chain reaction of criticism and defense ensues. Despite the numerous pleas for people to be kind to others scattered across the internet, my message is this: start by being kind to yourself. That's the real key. Cherish who you are, who you're becoming, and who you aim to be. Shower that person with love and patience. Once you have love for yourself, you can genuinely extend it to others. You can't give to others what you don't possess yourself.

If you're devoid of money, you can't offer it to someone else. If you lack water, you can't provide it to someone in need, no matter how much they need it or how badly you wish to give. Without genuine patience and love for yourself, any love you give is merely temporary or conditional. While many parents assert that they love their children more than themselves, thinking it is a noble sentiment, I challenge them: Can you present an example of inner peace, self-love, and self-worth? Can you refrain from calling yourself dumb, lazy, or unattractive? Let your children learn self-love without personal judgment. Let them inherit this liberating skill from you. Then your love for them becomes boundless, and they too can love without limit.

Be patient and kind to yourself. Celebrate your journey instead of berating yourself for not already reaching the destination.

## Mastering Choice Architecture

Decision fatigue sets in, even when we know better. I shouldn't order out tonight. I shouldn't buy that hat, because I already have so many. But we are bombarded with ads every day from the moment we wake up. The average person sees/ hears between six thousand to ten thousand ads per day.[8] From the instant we look at our phone in the morning, to turning on the radio in the car, to billboards, bench signs, or opening our email. Even our packages come with ads placed inside the box. We are bombarded with ads, and every time we do not act or buy, we are saying no. It is understandable that we don't experience the remorse we think we should when making an "impulse" buy. Was it an impulse buy, if I've been saying no all day, to the tune of six thousand times?

I don't say this to give us a pass, but rather to give us all some context. Too much advice from financial gurus comes with an air of judgment. It's never that simple or that easy, but the better we understand the forces that shape our mental state, the more successful we can be going forward. You can overcome decision fatigue by becoming the decision architect of your life. Create an environment where you are more likely to succeed than fail. James Clear refers to this as being a choice architect.[9] If you aim to make your body healthier, remove excessively sugary foods like soda and desserts from your home. That way, when your will falters, you can't eat the brownie if it's not in your house.

---

[8] Sam Carr, "How Many Ads Do We See a Day in 2024?" Lunio, https://lunio.ai/ blog/strategy/how-many-ads-do-we-see-a-day/.

[9] Clear, James. *Atomic Habits: An Easy & Proven Way to Buil, Goo, Habits & Break Ba, Ones* (New York: Avery, an imprint of Penguin Random House, 2018).

If you find that sleeping in prevents you from starting the day early, design your evening routine to ensure an early start. Go to bed early and place an alarm across the room. In the morning, you'll need to cross the cold floor to turn it off, making it less tempting to crawl back into bed.

If spending time with a lavish friend compromises your financial goals, perhaps reconsider those weekly fancy dinners and clubbing. Create the same bond with activities that align more with your objectives. Instead, choose activities that let you maintain your friendship without compromising your financial progress.

Ray Dalio, one of the world's most successful hedge fund managers, exemplifies the role of a choice architect. He refines his investment choices for optimal success through rigorous research and the application of his principles. Ray only enters positions where he knows that he can make wrong investment decisions three out of five times, and he and his clients will still profit. His decisions are structured so that even if he's right only once out of five times, he breaks even. This approach embodies the essence of a choice architecture, crafting an environment where success is more likely than failure.

Position yourself for success. Avoid situations or environments where failure is more probable than success. Being prepared for opportunities, choosing the right company, and understanding investment strategies to minimize risks and maximize gains are all crucial. Even if your decisions are wrong most of the time, structure them so that the wins outweigh the losses. You might be asking yourself why Ray's not aiming to be right five out of five times. He is, except his decisions are not based on the potential for gains; his investment choices are based on not losing money for his clients. He's creating an environment void of chances to experience losses.

This reminds me of a twenty-year-old pitcher for the Chicago Cubs. On Wednesday, May sixth, 1998, a young pitcher took the mound at historic Wrigley Field for the fifth start in his rookie season. Having received feedback both in the minors and in his earlier starts about his number of walks, this young man was singularly focused on one thing: not walking anyone. The baby-faced pitcher did not set out to throw a perfect game, nor did he set out to strike out every batter. His focus was on not throwing balls because he did not want to walk anyone. In the process Kerry Wood pitched the full nine innings and struck out twenty Houston Astros. On that overcast day Kerry achieved his gains (strikeouts) by painting all over that strike zone with precision and not throwing balls.

Kerry Wood's spectacular outcome appeared to be focused on a pitcher's offense (getting strikes), but his focus that afternoon was defensive and not throwing balls.

## Transitioning from Problem State to Solution State

We often spend too much time in what I call the "problem state"—letting issues persist mainly because addressing them feels uncomfortable. This problem state prevents you from aligning consistently with your goals and purpose. Problems are essentially inefficiencies that slow your progress and growth. If you allow too many problems to accumulate, your own operating systems may become unreliable or might even break down entirely.

By addressing and resolving these problems, you can boost your learning curve and enhance your skills and abilities to detect, correct, and even prevent future problems. You might believe that by sidestepping an issue, you're being a team player and avoiding unnecessary conflict. However, you're just exacerbating what's holding you back. Instead of tackling your problems directly, your hard work gets diverted toward circumventing or compensating for them. You end up spinning your wheels in the mud. Look around. You'll see others achieving immense success and satisfaction. Then, when you reflect on your own journey, you might wonder why you're not advancing, despite all your hard work.

Some prefer to hold on to their problems because it gives them a convenient excuse for not reaching their desired goals. The problem becomes a crutch, an integral part of their narrative of struggle. Don't embrace or fall in love with your problems.

Choose to see them differently and overcome them. The story of your journey should not be about all the things that held you back in life. Instead, the story of your journey should be about the person you've become as you learned from all the challenges you overcame.

## The Distinction between Amateurs and Professionals

Drawing inspiration from James Clear, it's evident that the journey to mastery is paved with consistent effort. The question is: who can endure the monotony of training, day in and day out? Achieving mastery is synonymous with relentless practice. The most significant barrier to success isn't necessarily failure but rather boredom. True success means showing up, even when it's tedious, uncomfortable, or downright dull.

Professionals adhere to their routines, regardless of external distractions. In contrast, amateurs allow life's unpredictable events to derail their commitments. Take professional athletes and actors, for instance. It's easy to say they're in impeccable shape because they're paid to be, and that's precisely the point. Being in top physical condition is part and parcel of their profession, so they commit to it, working out even when the motivation wanes, because it's their job, their responsibility. Their compensation and lifestyle are directly impacted if they don't remain in that top physical condition. How's that for a motivator?

My sister Susy, who's had two, if not three, jobs for most of her working life, thrives on challenges and keeping herself going. I can remember a time when I thought she had picked up weightlifting as an interest. However, it turned out she took on a part-time job at a local gym and was teaching six fitness classes a week. She was in the best shape of her life and getting paid to do so. If your aim is to be in great shape, find a job that incentivizes regular exercise. If you're passionate about culinary arts, immerse yourself in a professional kitchen.

Remember, true mastery or transformation isn't the result of one significant act or shift, but the culmination of countless small improvements. Embrace and fall in love with the process, as that's where true growth lies.

## Embrace the Power of Being Unreasonable

You must be unreasonable, unyielding, unrelenting, and unmerciful when it comes to protecting and providing for your future and your family's future. I can guide you, but many of you won't follow through because you are too reasonable. Mastery stems from unreasonableness. Olympians, professional athletes, and those at the pinnacle of their professions reach such heights precisely because they're unreasonable. They didn't listen to the voices telling them they weren't good enough. Crucially, many of these discouraging voices were their own internal monologues. To achieve greatness, you must be unreasonable.

Being unreasonable does not mean being stubborn without a plan or preparation. That would be like expecting to surf a one-hundred-foot wave successfully, without a tow or rescue team on hand. Being unreasonable means you have the courage to challenge yourself, the strength to ignore the naysayers, and the will to push beyond pain and setbacks.

## You Must Embody What You Seek

When you look at people who have reached the highest levels of success—be it Olympians, military generals, renowned doctors, or global movie stars—know they did not receive their coronation and suddenly decide to carry themselves in a different manner and hold themselves to a higher standard. To the contrary, their eventual crowning moment happened because decades before, they chose to hold themselves to that higher standard.

If you want to achieve financial success, then you have to manage your money as if you already have achieved the level of success you want. The very wealthy spend less than they make. Find a way to save. Make purchases that advance you in the direction that you want to move in, not purchases that feed your ego. If financial success is your aim, manage your resources as if you've already achieved it. Notably, the affluent consistently spend below their means and prioritize savings. Their purchases align with their ambitions, not just to satisfy fleeting desires or impress friends. Oprah Winfrey, for instance, didn't wait for her financial pinnacle to adopt the demeanor of a CEO. She embraced her identity early on, guiding her through life's highs, lows, and complexities, propelling her toward unparalleled success.

Similarly, a military general doesn't adopt honor only after attaining his rank. To truly thrive, you must first have a crystal-clear vision of your aspirations and conduct yourself as if you've already realized them. That's when life truly becomes exhilarating, accelerating your path to success. Recognize and cherish your unique brilliance even before the world takes notice. If you await external validation to affirm your worth, the journey ahead will be longer and harder.

## Embrace Your Unique Strengths

We all have a very funny friend or family member. You're probably thinking of them now. They are absolutely and consistently hilarious despite never having been trained or having gone through comedy or acting school. They have spent their life subconsciously sharpening that comedic "knife" because it came naturally to them. At some point in life, they received positive feedback, or it helped them survive a dangerous situation, and they've been sharpening that skill ever since. Maybe you're the funny friend everyone raves about, but you downplay your talent because it's never felt like work for you. Being funny has always come naturally to you.

Similarly, too often, what we perceive as our "weakness" can be our greatest asset—a distinguishing feature that sets us apart in a crowded world. Growing up in diverse environments—whether it's in a disadvantaged neighborhood or within multiple cultures—can shape us in unique ways. While we readily admire and praise others for their talents, saying, "They're truly exceptional in what they do," we tend to undervalue our own abilities, brushing them off as commonplace. But the reality is not everyone possesses your unique blend of skills, experiences, and perspectives.

Your life's journey, marked by efforts to compensate, adapt, and sometimes even hide your perceived weaknesses, has made you a master in that very domain. When you acknowledge and embrace this, you tap into a strength and skill that is unparalleled.

## Just Get Started

Tony Robbins articulates that there are five elements to what he calls the chemistry of change. The first element is *satiation.* This is where you've eaten so much of your favorite rich, indulgent dessert that even though there's a full buffet of dessert available, you simply cannot take another bite. You are past the level of being satisfied and nearing the brink of getting sick. The second element is *dissatisfaction*, and this is where you are plainly unhappy, and you can't convince yourself otherwise.

You can't talk your way into feeling better about the situation you are in. The next element is *threshol*. You are officially fed up and are up to the brink of what you can tolerate. Just past threshold is *insight*. Here is where you are open to alternative ideas and radical change. The fifth element is the open window for change. If you fail to move and take action, the fifth element closes. This is what is known as striking the iron while it's hot.

You want to be mentally prepared, understanding the pitfalls and challenges of the landscape as well as the often contradicting psychology that we bring to the table. So, when the window opens, you seize the opportunity for change. Failing to do so resets everything. You won't reach the window opening again until you've experienced satiation, dissatisfaction, broken through threshold, and you've found different insight again.

Does this feel or sound familiar? Where you finally left a job or a relationship, and you can't believe how easy it was to do once you made up your mind. Then you ask yourself, if it was this easy and clear now, why didn't I do this sooner? The answer is because you had not arrived at threshold, then insight. Most people won't adopt change until the pain is big enough. You don't have to operate this way. Don't allow judgment to get in the way of your growth.

You've likely heard that canned vegetables lack nutritional value because they're packed with additives. People say frozen vegetables aren't as good as fresh ones and that most fresh vegetables are laden with pesticides. Do you see the pattern? Every starting point is judged. We can become so engrossed in determining what's best that we never begin, as the debate seems endless. The truth is, canned vegetables are much better than no vegetables at all. Frozen veggies are preferable to wilted ones, and while fresh vegetables are ideal, they aren't necessary to begin your journey. Some budget cuts and even modest savings are far better than no cuts or no savings at all. So, don't judge yourself or your journey. Choose to start today and celebrate your progress.

You woke up this morning and already have everything you need. Look at all the tools, assets, and blessings around you. Maybe you are blinded by what you don't have. Or maybe you can't see your blessings and opportunities because you've buried yourself financially by trying to chase social media's representation of success. That's okay. Take a moment to breathe and look carefully and patiently. If you see even a tiny glint of one tool, that's an excellent start.

Decide, in this moment, to stop chasing what other people define as success. Instead, choose to walk with confidence and conviction toward your own definition of success.

## The Hero's Inner Journey

Joseph Campbell breaks down the hero's journey with scientific precision. The hero begins as naïve, bumbling, and insecure. Then they are faced with a life-altering problem. The hero leaves home, feeling and believing they are unworthy of love from their family/community. The hero declares: "I will not return home until I succeed, and they will all see me for who I am." The hero embarks on a journey to avenge or overcome this problem, and in the process, transforms into a hero. Many additional challenges will lie in the path of the hero's journey. The hero will meet an older, wiser, and more experienced mentor. The mentor will guide the hero to find the answers within. Ultimately, the hero reaches the pinnacle of success by defeating the enemy, avenging their family, or achieving world-renowned success and acclaim.

The hero has status and praise from people who want something in return. The hero discovers they are surrounded by strangers. The hero returns home to their family. The hero returns to the people who knew and loved them before their journey, transformation, and triumph. These are the people who loved the hero just for merely existing. Many times over, we've read about the hero's journey in books and watched it in movies. The warm feeling of love and acceptance envelopes the hero, and a moment of discovery comes over them. They had this love and acceptance all along. They did not need to leave home, risk it all, scale that mountain, or slay any dragons. The journey wasn't the hero against the world, but the hero against their perceived insecurities, which prevented them from allowing and receiving the acceptance they craved from those they loved.

They are searching for a reason to believe that they are worthy and deserving of their own love and the love of others. Once the hero discovers how to love themselves, the world changes instantly, even though nothing has changed. Only now can the hero truly love another because they learned to love themselves first. The hero can accept love from others and teach them by example how to love themselves.

Growth is important and essential. You can fast-track your journey by recognizing that all you need in life is already within you. With or without talent. Once you reach your ultimate purpose, it's game over. You're not working anymore; you're living. Along the way are the lessons, the learning, and the skill-building. You will make the decisions that delay your arrival or accelerate your journey.

# PART 3

# THE
# MECHANICAL STEPS TO CREATE FINANCIAL SECURITY

# Chapter 6

## Action Steps

### The Budget, Audit, and Monitor (B.A.M.) Formula

**From Crisis Living to Financial Harmony**

Carrying unsustainable debt often pushes individuals into what I term "crisis living." When faced with a financial emergency, many feel as if their back is against the wall, as if they have limited options beyond taking on more debt to cover expenses. Resorting to credit cards, cash loans, or payday loans only deepens the debt pit. Merely receiving a sudden cash influx won't rectify the fundamental issues in one's budget that led to the financial dilemma in the first place. This is why someone who was financially struggling before winning the lottery often finds themselves in a similar predicament shortly after their windfall.

The core issue is the lack of necessary tools and skills to manage finances effectively. Even a significant cash injection can't address these foundational problems. Millions of Americans remain trapped in this cycle of crisis, often for years on end. I aim for you to break free from crisis living and find a sense of harmony and balance in your financial life.

Emergencies are a part of life, affecting everyone regardless of income or background. The goal should be to structure your finances so that you can bounce back when setbacks occur. By managing your household income within specific guidelines, you can achieve this harmony and balance, giving you the capability to establish an emergency fund. Consequently, when emergencies arise, your budget has the flexibility to either absorb the shock or at least mitigate its effects.

Failing to adhere to these guidelines means you're constantly in a reactive mode, especially during financial emergencies. This reactive stance can make you feel trapped, believing your only way out is resorting to credit cards or quick loans, which only drags you back into crisis living.

## The Budget Process

### Strategic Budgeting for Success

To achieve financial stability, it's crucial to allocate your resources wisely. Here's a breakdown I recommend for budgeting:

- **Housing:** Allocate no more than 30% of your post-tax income. This is the amount you're left with after all taxes and deductions.

- **Transportation:** Set aside 15%, covering your car payments, insurance, and fuel.

- **Utilities:** Dedicate 15%.

- **Food:** Budget 16%.

- **Personal/Miscellaneous:** Allot 19%.

- **Debt Repayment:** If you're in debt, designate 5% for repayments.

For those without debt, the distribution may vary. However, for the purpose of this book, these percentages serve as a guiding framework.

Take a moment to evaluate your spending in these six core areas: housing, transportation, food, utilities, personal/miscellaneous, and debt. Compare your current expenses to these benchmarks. You might discover that while you're overspending in some categories, you're underspending in others, potentially balancing out your overall budget.

With these benchmarks in place, you now have a tangible reference to guide your spending, ensuring it's aligned with sound financial principles rather than arbitrary decisions.

### Breaking the Cycle of Arbitrary and Emotional Decisions

Many clients approach me after years of making financial choices based on emotion, impulse, or general advice found on social media. By using the budget guidelines outlined above, you can move beyond these hit-or-miss methods, tailoring financial strategies to your unique situation and goals. Gone are the days of arbitrary, emotion-driven decisions.

> *Limiting Financial Belief:* ***Everyone around me appears to be much further ahead financially than I am.*** – Feeling like you are behind is natural; social media is plastered with the façade of perfect lives. But this is far from reality. Looking like you have money is far different than knowing you have financial security.

### Personalized Financial Strategies

It's essential to remember that your financial journey is personal. For instance, if you discover from the guidelines that your housing expenses are too high, your next step might be to downsize your living situation or consider a roommate. Perhaps it's time to rethink the number of cars you own or consider alternative financing solutions. The key is to make choices tailored to your circumstances rather than mindlessly following generic advice or mimicking others.

As Warren Buffett wisely noted, you aren't right just because others agree with you; you're right because you've done your research and drawn informed conclusions.

## Mastering Cash Flow & Operating Costs

### Mapping Your Income

Begin with your earnings. Track every paycheck—yours, your spouse's, and even those working teenagers who pitch in. Account for rental incomes, benefits, or any other sources.

### Accuracy Is Key

Ensure your calculations are spot-on. Why? Because every dollar matters. If you receive the same paycheck amount bi-monthly, double it. Paid bi-weekly? Multiply by 2.17 or, alternately, multiply by 26 (the annual number of pay periods) and then divide by 12 to get your monthly earnings. Weekly earners should multiply their paychecks by 4.33. No rounding up or down. Precision is crucial.

Capture every expense. Track every expense, from the primary earners to teenagers and even youngsters with digital purchasing power. Cell phones, tablets, and video games are ingeniously crafted to easily separate you from your money.

### Establishing a Baseline

With your monthly income in focus, establish a consistent baseline, especially if your income fluctuate. This baseline represents the amount you can consistently rely on. Avoid planning around conditional or tentative incomes, which I dub as "ifcome." Your budget should be grounded in actual, solid income.

> *Limiting Financial Belief:* **I've never been good with money.**
> – It is understandable to feel this way, as I illustrate in this book, that many factors are working against our success. If you don't already have the financial success you dream of, it's not your fault. We do what we can with the tools that we have. I am providing you with tools to turn this mindset around.

### Adopt a Business Mindset

Consider this: Successful businesses meticulously track their recurring expenses and monitor their revenue streams. This data allows them to plan and anticipate. Businesses prepare for changes in the market and dips in revenue by boosting savings and reducing expenses. These changes are made monthly and quarterly, allowing a business to prepare for challenges instead of being left solely to react.

Equipped with a clear understanding of your monthly financial needs and expected income, you can plan and anticipate. Knowledge is empowerment. By knowing your precise needs, you're poised to make strategic financial decisions.

### Know Your Expenses Inside Out

When I ask my clients how much they spend per month on housing, most can quote their rent or mortgage down to the last cent. The same goes for car payments or utility bills. When I ask them how much all of these expenses are, per month, combined, that's when the blank stare comes in. Learning what it costs to operate their household every month is vital.

Break down and tally up your monthly expenditures. Account for everything from mortgages and utilities to student loans and medical bills. Knowing this total is pivotal.

### Your Cash Flow: An Overview

Subtracting your monthly operating expenses from your income gives you your cash flow. Ideally, you want this to be positive. If, for instance, you earn $5,600 a month but spend $5,400, your cash flow stands at a modest $200. That narrow safety net offers limited flexibility for unexpected expenses or indulgences.

While many sense they have a tight budget, they prefer not to look under the bed out of fear that the upside-down budget monster will really be there. You can fix a tight and even upside-down budget but, you must be acutely aware of your cash flow. Refusing to look under the bed will not make the budget monster disappear. Know your cash flow.

### *Budget for Maintenance, Emergencies, and Repairs*

Most expensive purchases require not only repairs at the time but also regular maintenance. Dedicate a section of your monthly budget for maintenance, emergencies, and repairs. Here are some events that affect both homeowners and renters, albeit a little differently.

### *Homeowners*

Homeowners must budget for significant appliance repairs such as washing machines, dryers, and refrigerators. These items may need to be repaired or replaced. The likelihood of this occurring is greater the closer you reach their tenth-anniversary date. Consider how long you've had an appliance when planning how much to set aside monthly. A fifteen-hundred-dollar emergency sucks when you have the savings and are prepared. But if you are unprepared, a fifteen-hundred-dollar emergency could start the snowball effect of falling into debt or be the tipping point of compounding debt.

Heating and air-conditioning systems can last twenty years or longer. Still, they require regular maintenance and occasional repair, which could cost hundreds of dollars.

Plumbing is behind the walls, and your garage and home roofs get little foot traffic, but they will turn your life upside down if they don't perform as intended. Be aware of the age of your heating, plumbing, and roofs as you decide to put money aside for emergency repairs.

Landscape costs, lawncare machinery, and equipment can be significant. Setting aside just $25 per week for this area of your homecare can go a long way in offsetting the cost of replacing a lawn mower or paying for a desired backyard project.

### Renters

Renters don't have to worry about landscaping, roof repairs, or general plumbing. Still, some items that are important fall in a renter's field. Kitchen appliances can break down with use and may need replacing. Your personal electronics, such as laptops, cell phones, and TVs, can be expensive to replace. Set aside some savings for your next upgrade.

Renters tend to move more frequently than homeowners. Be aware that you are not promised a 100% security deposit return. Build savings for a future security deposit on your next place.

Additionally, set up a personal budget for replacement furniture. Not every desk, dresser, or couch will follow you to your next apartment. Having a "reset" budget will make your next move not only more affordable but also less stressful.

### Everyone

Vehicles are not exclusive to homeowners or renters; many Americans don't have cars. That being said, according to the Federal Highway Administration, in 2019, there were 253 million licensed drivers.The better you maintain your vehicle with regular oil changes, tire rotations, brake inspections, and tune-ups, the less likely you will encounter a significant car repair. The older your car, the more likely it is to need more extensive repairs. Set a goal to set aside $150 per month for repairs and maintenance. If you are hit with a car emergency, you will have $1,800 from one year of savings. Setting aside funds for unforeseen circumstances is wise. But for long-term stability, especially from a young age to retirement, building these savings habits is vital.

### A Budget Keeps You on Target

Budgets are neither fun nor sexy, but they are the best way to measure and monitor where your money is going. If you measure, you will know if your expenses are increasing, decreasing, or ballooning and by how much. If you are not measuring, you cannot monitor. Measuring your cash flow, which is the money you have left over every month after your expenses, helps your ability to save. Not saving adequately exposes you to financial emergencies and leaves you with fewer options when these events occur.

Having a budget is just the beginning. You want to implement an audit to truly understand and control your finances. An audit can be transformative.

## The Audit Process

An audit transforms you from a passive to an active participant. Every championship team has a good offense, and equally, if not more important, is the need for a strong defense. To be a financial champion, you must implement the same high-level strategies into your financial game plan. It is not enough to make money. You have to be absolutely defensive with your money. The harsh reality is that if you don't make plans for your money someone else will. Think of all the times on a daily and weekly, if not monthly, basis that money slips through your hands because you have yet to assign your money a task or destination.

You wouldn't use your mortgage money to buy new furniture. You know not to touch that money. You have assigned your mortgage money to your mortgage. Yet, we unconsciously allow "unassigned" money to leave our hands. This defensive strategy is designed to empower you and help you stop others from taking your hard-earned money. I provide my clients with tools and strategies to self-audit their spending. The results are transformative.

The audit process itself is an incredibly useful tool. I will show you how to use this process and audit your service providers. When I say audit, most people imagine an IRS agent combing through receipts and tax forms to find ways to make you pay more taxes.

With this process, you will do the audit to ensure you are not overpaying or being charged more than you should.

### Step 1. Gather All Your Monthly Statements.

Any lender or service provider who sends you a monthly statement will be audited. This includes your mortgage, car loan, credit card, loan statements, utilities, cell phone, and even bank statements. The goal of this process is to go through each individual statement line by line.

### Step 2. Check for Convenience Fees

You will look for fees that don't apply to you. For example, you may find a service fee of $6 per month on your internet bill.

When you call the provider and ask about this "service fee," they apologize, say the fee doesn't apply to your account, and offer to remove it. Great! While deducting the fee, they can also reimburse you for all the months they charged you this fee in error.

There will likely be some policy where they can only go back so far regarding refunds. Still, you can encourage them to provide you with a credit on your account. If they don't remove the fee, press them hard for a detailed explanation of why they are entitled to it. You can always take your business to a competitor.

You may find similar service fees on your bank statement. Such a service fee may be $15 or $25, applied monthly when certain deposits still need to be met or a certain number of checks written have exceeded set levels. You want to call and find out the details of this fee. You want to learn how you can have it removed today and how you can avoid it in the future. The idea is that you will not be passive about getting hit over the head with fees. You will be proactive and build up a defensive line that your service providers will need to break through if they want to access your money.

### Cancel Anytime Offers

I see this a lot, doing this process with my clients. My clients had agreed to a monthly subscription years ago and have since stopped using the service or forgotten they were being billed month after month.

The cable provider often offers you a channel package with premium channels and says it's free for the first three months. The cable company hopes you'll love the channels so much that after three months, you won't call to cancel. They are also hoping that in the event you want to cancel, you won't remember.

In this process, they will get to bill you for a couple extra months they otherwise would not have been able to, if they had not offered you a free trial. They often bill you for months or years for a channel lineup you don't want.

The point here is to be aware of how these free trials work. When you agree to a free trial, let your defense know you'll have some money to protect in the coming months.

### How to Make Cuts

Look at your cable bill. Are you using everything you are paying for? Can you trim it down? Do you stream most of your viewing anyway? I have seen thousands of client cable TV bills, most of which were in the $200-$300 range per month.

If you cut that bill by one-third, you would have some serious money back in your budget for paying down debt or building your savings.

### Separating Us from Our Money

Credit card companies are incredibly resourceful and creative in getting us to use their products.

They also know how to desensitize us to separating us and our money. Paying for something with cash is a transaction where money leaves you and goes to someone else. There is a visceral feeling when that money leaves your hands.

There is energy in that paper money and energy in that transaction. Think about when you pay with your credit card.

Do you have the same instinct or feeling of wow, this is expensive, or wow, there goes all my money? No, it's just a swipe of a three-inch piece of plastic with a magnetic strip. There's no energy and no emotion.

Right there, the credit card companies have won. They have separated us from our money without pain, emotion, or anxiety.

In the same way, they have conditioned us to see a balance creep on a credit card statement. They will slip in their fees and services, expecting that you will not notice the fee before paying it each month.

> *Limiting Financial Belief:* ***There are so many different stocks that investing feels overwhelming.*** There are many talking heads on TV and social media overcomplicating for the sake of taking their piece of the pie. Understanding market principles will help you sniff out the BS. See Financial Relationships – supply and demand. Stocks aren't your only option; there are many different options to help your money grow.

### *Make Your Money Work for You*

If, in your audit process, you discover that you are getting hit regularly with late payment fees, call your credit card company. Call and ask them to move your due date to a day when you know you will have funds available to pay without missing the deadline and without getting hit with that $35 late fee.

I have seen countless times on my client's credit card statements that the company charges them for a credit guard service. I am not a fan of paying for credit guard services. Firstly, monitoring your credit is something you can do on your own and for free.

Secondly, the protection offered by this guard service is already built into the credit card.

You're not gaining any additional protection. If someone steals your identity and runs up your credit card, you don't need a "credit guard" to protect you. If you dispute the fraud with your credit card company, you may need a police report, but the matter is resolved. So, why pay $10 monthly for a service you don't need or use?

I have seen clients with multiple credit cards from this one major credit card company . . . I won't name names. All are issued with low credit limits of $250. Each month, the client was being charged a $10 credit guard, $35 over the limit, and a $35 late fee. My clients had clearly reached the max amount, yet their credit card was still growing by $80 in fees every month.

This, of course, did not include the interest being charged by the bank on the growing balance. I remember one couple I met with had four cards like this. Every month their debt level grew by $320, just in fees alone.

Fees are big business. Let's go back in time. Before streaming giants Netflix and Hulu became a part of our everyday lives, if you wanted to see a movie at home, you had to walk into a video store and rent a physical VHS cassette or DVD. In those days, no one had more market share than Blockbuster Video. Blockbuster rented videos, sold popcorn and candy, and made money by renting you Hollywood's biggest hits. Yet, Blockbuster didn't just make money on renting you the movies; they also made money on late fees. In 2000, Blockbuster brought in nearly eight hundred million dollars in late fees alone.

This accounted for nearly 16% of their revenue. Despite the added cost and pain to the consumer, Blockbuster had eight hundred million reasons motivating them not to change their late fee structure.

In 2016, credit card companies disclosed they brought in twelve billion dollars in penalty fees. Twelve billion dollars is a lot of money; this differs from the change you find in your couch. The landscape of the American economy would shift dramatically if consumers could use the same twelve billion dollars to stimulate the economy and not line the pockets of a few bank executives. Could twelve billion dollars have helped homeowners during the real estate crash of 2008? Could the support of the middle class have helped our economy recover and grow?

My point is that industries are built on and thrive on taking money from you without you noticing. I have no issue with a business charging an appropriate fee for quality service or a product. My issue is with a company that purposely designs ways to trick, confuse, and mislead you into walking away from more of your money via fees. If you don't make plans for your money, someone else will. We have to be smarter with our money, individually and collectively.

You are going to audit each and every monthly statement. You will find $3 savings in some and $60 in others. The process continues beyond bringing these funds back into your budget.

Step 3. Give Each Dollar a Job

Once you have brought this money back, you must give it a task, a job. You will assign each dollar you get back into your budget to pay down your debt or build your savings. You must make this money work for you.

I see online ads by "experts," offering to sell you a course to teach you how to "make your money work for you." You don't need to buy that course. You don't have to be a real estate wizard or stock market guru. By completing this process, you will make your money, get off the couch, and go to work, paying down your debt and building your savings.

## The Monitor Process

*Lighting Your Pathway to a Deserved Lifestyle*

I've covered how to develop and deploy the defense needed to protect your money. Now, I'll guide you in crafting a championship-caliber offense.

You want to meticulously record every expense you incur for the next two weeks. It's crucial here: don't cut corners. Spend and consume as you usually would. For instance, if you pay your mortgage on a Tuesday, fill your gas tank, and write a check for a school fundraiser, record all these outflows. The aim is to capture a genuine snapshot of your spending habits.

Consider your morning commute. Do you grab something at the drive-thru en route to work? When you refuel your car, do you also pick up a bottle of water, candy, or lotto tickets? You need a genuine representation of your spending habits. Document every expense without self-judgment. If you hesitate over an impulse-buy at the store, thinking about recording it later, go ahead and buy it. Don't modify your behavior during this tracking phase; otherwise, you'll skew the data you collect. Document your expenses and those of anyone in your household with spending power.

After the two-week period, review all your expenses. Now, you can critically assess every item on that worksheet. Categorize your expenses as necessities or conveniences. We often splurge on convenience. While you must eat, dining out four times a week isn't essential. Distinguish between such expenses.

### Time to Trim

By merely halving your convenience expenses, you'll reclaim significant funds in your budget, which can be channeled toward paying down debt and building your savings. This strategy puts you in command of your finances and optimizes your financial offense.

### Elevating Your Lifestyle

Financial pundits often chastise daily luxuries like coffee shop lattes. Have you ever heard that if you saved the cost of a daily latte from age twenty-one to sixty-five with 10% compound interest, you'd retire a millionaire? But let's not pick on coffee shops. Suppose that latte genuinely enhances your day? You shouldn't have to forsake it.

Perhaps that morning coffee ritual is a cherished reward, symbolizing your hard work. If so, savor it without remorse. You'll likely spot other, less meaningful expenditures through this monitor process. Maybe you dine out too often for lunch. Preparing a homemade lunch is both healthier and more economical. Plus, you're probably tired of the same old lunch spots.

Keep revisiting and refining this process. Eliminate expenditures that don't enrich your life and keep those that make your hard work feel worthwhile. As you make these adjustments, you'll bring money back into your budget. And yes, you'll use these dollars to pay down your debt and increase your savings.

## How to Pay Down Debt

If you're going to succeed long-term, you can't build real wealth while you're still paying down debt or, worse, paying your debt with no progress.

Get your building blocks in place and build your financial empire. You can't pay down debt if you don't have a surplus in your budget, or worse if you don't know if you have a surplus.

The only way to pay off debt is with income.

Repeat after me. *The only way to pay off debt is with income.*

Too many industries thrive on shuffling your debt around and taking your money. Industry traps include refinancing, cash advances, payday loans, emergency cash, personal loans, consolidation, and debt management plans. Every magic pill listed above has its side effect. It's going to cost you money, it's going to cost you time, or it's going to cost you credit. You must be aware of which of these three you are willing to sacrifice.

### The Wrong Strategy

I will show you how to pay down your mortgage, car, student loans, credit cards, and other miscellaneous debt. How do you pay this down in the cheapest and fastest way possible? You will pay it down with the income you bring home today without working overtime or a second job. You achieve this by taking control of every dollar that comes into your household.

We all know and understand that you cannot send just the minimum payment to the credit card companies; you'll never get out of debt and never finish paying it off. So, what is the best strategy to pay down your debt? If I approach my family and ask one uncle, he will say you want to pay down the credit card with the highest balance first. If I ask another uncle (I had thirteen to choose from), he would say to pay down the card with the lowest minimum payment. Everyone has a different formula or recipe, and they are all getting it wrong. This is perfectly fine with the lending industry, of course. They are content with us not knowing the most efficient strategy to get out of debt because it makes them more money.

### The Winning Strategy

Let's look at how our ancestors paid down their credit card debt. From the beginning, whenever they would bring home extra money, they'd say: Honey, I got a bonus this week; let's send extra money to the credit cards. They would send $5, $10, and $25 extra to each card. How did that work out for them? Not too well.

Let me propose this differently. Let's say you are trying to convince everyone in the United States that you have the number one candidate for the job. You've been given a limited number of resources to accomplish this goal. You have just one hundred volunteers. We take our one hundred volunteers and spread them out across the border of the United States and begin to have conversations, discussions, blog posts, town meetings, and even a couple bar fights. Is this the most efficient use of our limited resources?

Not at all. This is an inefficient use of our resources, and we are spreading ourselves too thin. We're trying to be everywhere at once. This is precisely what we do when we send $5, $10, and $25 extra to our creditors.

If we're trying to be everywhere at once, ultimately, we will lose our campaign, and we don't want that to happen.

Let me show you a strategy that is much more efficient. When working with so few resources, you want to pick one state and begin your campaign. That begs the question, where are we going to start? We will gather all our resources and begin in America's great northwest; we begin in Washington and, from there, begin our conversations and debates. Before you know it, we've picked up some more volunteers and moved on to the next state. Now, we're in Oregon and starting to pick up some momentum. By the time we hit Idaho, we're charging full steam ahead.

This is precisely the same strategy you want to implement when we're going after our creditors and trying to pay down debt.

Many years ago, I worked with a couple, and I will share the payment strategy breakdown we prepared for them. We sat down with this couple and did all the previous steps together. We did their budget, audit, and monitor process, and we found $100 in their monthly surplus income that we could make work for them; those are the one hundred volunteers they would put toward paying down their debt.

DEBT REDUCTION PAYMENT = $100

| CREDITOR | PRSENT BALANCE | MONTLHY PAYMENT | MONTHS TO PAYOFF | PAYOFF PRIORITY | DEBT RED. PAYMENT | NEW PLAN MONTHS TO PAY OFF |
|---|---|---|---|---|---|---|
| Discover | $1,250 | $26 | 84 | 4 | $310 | 4 |
| Auto Loan | $5,843 | $121 | 48 | 3 | $284 | 21 |
| Store Card 2 | $1,306 | $27 | 48 | 2 | $163 | 8 |
| Store Card 1 | $986 | $19 | 52 | 5 | $329 | 3 |
| 2nd Mortgage | $39,360 | $356 | 111 | 9 | $758 | 52 |
| 3rd Mortgage | $1,372 | $21 | 65 | 7 | $374 | 4 |
| Student Loan | $1,250 | $24 | 52 | 6 | $353 | 4 |
| Visa 1 | $2,341 | $28 | 84 | 8 | $402 | 6 |
| Mastercard | $1,750 | $36 | 47 | 1 | $136 | 13 |
| 1st Mortgage | $123,530 | $822 | 150 | 10 | $1,580 | 78 |

The table has seven columns from left to right, and the rows on the spreadsheet are based on how many actual creditors you have. In the first column, you list all your creditors, and creditors are precisely those you owe money to; this includes your mortgage, car, student loans, and credit cards; this is not for your living expenses like food and utilities. This couple owed nearly $180,000 and spent $1,500 a month, including a first mortgage, a second mortgage, a third mortgage, a car loan, and student loans.

In the second column, you will list the balances owed on these debts as they appear on your monthly statement.

The one hundred volunteers we're able to find through the budget, audit and monitor process is what we will use to accelerate our debt payment strategy.

In the third column, you will also list the minimum monthly payments as provided on your monthly statements.

In this instance, the Discover card has a minimum payment of $26. Repeat this step all the way down to the mortgage. This couple is walking away from $1480 every month. Remember, this is only to pay down their debt; again, this does not include their living expenses.

This means they're walking away from $1500 every month that they will never see again, just to pay down debt.

We need to figure out how long it will take to pay off these creditors. We will start with Discover; we will divide the balance of $1250 by the minimum payment of $26 and an ultimate number of forty-eight months to pay off this debt. You will repeat this step with all the debt. Lastly, we learn that the debt that takes the longest to pay off is the mortgage at 150 months.

The debt that gets paid off fastest is the MasterCard at forty-seven months.

I'm showing you how to do this with pen and paper, so you can do this at home, at your kitchen table. You can teach your brother, your sister, and your child in college how they, too, can get out of debt and stay out of debt.

By doing the calculations on paper, we compare all debts on the same scale. We're comparing apples to apples and oranges to oranges.

Why does it matter which debt you start this strategy with? When we begin any journey, we want to see progress. When you create a new workout routine, you want to see results. When you start a new diet, you want to see results. We start with the debt you will pay off soon so you begin to see results. If we start with the debt that takes the longest, you will not see the momentum, and you might be inclined to stop altogether.

This is why we set the priority for you to pay off your debts in this specific order.

To begin, we will take our one hundred volunteers and add them to our $36 minimum payment to the MasterCard. The new debt reduction payment is now $136. Instead of paying off this debt in nearly four years, they are paying it off in one month more than one year, just thirteen months.

Remember that the only way we can continue to add $100 to this minimum payment is by sending the minimum payments only, to all other creditors. If we start sending an extra $15 here, $25 there, we're going to lose those one hundred volunteers. We have to stay focused, and most people freak out when I tell them that everyone else gets the minimum. We're fast-tracking this process, and while you have a process and the strategy in place, don't worry about the other accounts. Continue to send the minimum so we pay off this debt in just thirteen months.

After we pay off the first debt, we move on to debt priority number two. That's the store card. Instead of paying off the card in forty-eight months, they are now set to pay off the card in eight months. That has a minimum payment of $27. We will add the $136 ($100 volunteers plus MasterCard payment) to the $27 and get a monthly payment of $163.

Let me take a step back before we move on to debt number two. What do we do as consumers when we pay off a debt? We are very creative creatures. We'll say, "Honey, the car will be paid off in September; time to buy a new car." Almost as if we're allergic to our money, and we want to keep it away from us. We immediately find someplace else to spend it. "Honey, it's time to get that swimming pool or buy a car for Jr."

While you're in the plan, there will be no new spending. When you pay something off, you will return the money to your budget and roll it into the next debt.

Now, back to our regularly scheduled paydown strategy.

Once they paid off the MasterCard, they moved on to debt #2 and paid off the store card in just eight months.

Next, they take that extra $163 and add it to debt #3, which is the car. The car payment is $121; once they add the $163, the new accelerated payment is $284, and the car is paid off, not in forty-eight months but just twenty-one months.

Then, we get to debt number four and repeat the same process. We get to debt number five; we're making some progress, and suddenly, a financial emergency happens.

Let's say your car breaks down, and the radiator is the issue. This is going to require a $600 repair. What is this couple going to do? How will they pay for this emergency?

Let's take a look at where they are. They are on debt number five and send this creditor $329 monthly.

The regular monthly payment is just $19.

$329-$19 = an instant emergency fund of $310, simply by having the discipline to be in this plan.

I just told you that we're not creating any new debt while inside this paydown plan, but if you don't have the $600 for the repair in savings, you will need to use a credit card.

For the next two months, your payment plan is on pause. You will send just the $19 to the creditor and use the $310 emergency savings to pay off the new car expense, which was charged to the card. In the third month, you will resume your payment plan and return to send the creditor $329 a month.

You need to get the car fixed to get to work. You need to get to work to get paid. If you get paid, you'll keep your house. If you keep your house, you'll keep your cool. So, you want to pay for the repair and get back on track.

Stay calm during the temporary interruption of this plan. Remember your original track to pay off this debt; the mortgage, car, student loans, and the rest was thirty years long. Using this strategy, we're reducing that time by fifteen years or more. Extending your paydown plan by two months means you might add two months to fifteen years, not two months to the thirty-year timeline.

You paid off the car repairs, and now we're back on track to continue paying off debt number five, and you're sending the $329 per month. You will repeat this process to pay off debts six, seven, eight, and nine. Now, we get down to debt number ten. Currently, the couple is sending $1580 to the mortgage company. How did we get to this number?

Remember, at the beginning of this plan, this couple sent their creditors $1480 every month; we added one hundred volunteers, which brought us up to $1580 monthly.

The original mortgage payment is $822. This money is for the principal and interest only. It does not include the escrow or taxes and insurance. Why? Remember, once you pay off your house, you will still have to pay taxes and insurance on the property into infinity.

We want to avoid inflating the mortgage payment in the plan by including the escrow amount. We'll only have the principal and interest related to paying the loan.

With the new accelerated payment, this couple could pay off the thirty-year mortgage in seventy-eight months.

For all my math majors, that's just six and a half years.

How valuable would this information be for a first-time home buyer? Wouldn't it be fantastic if you could return and give yourself this education twenty years ago?

Here's the best part! If you are fifty-five and just recently took on a new mortgage, you now have the tools you need to pay off your mortgage in seven years or less, and you won't have to carry your mortgage into retirement.

If you're fifty-five and have adult children, show them the way. Help them avoid the pain, stress, and struggles of wrestling with debt.

Start your legacy today.

Build them up to be stronger than you were at their age.

I'll remind you, this couple could pay off all their debt with the money they brought home. They did not have to work overtime or get a second job. They did not have to chase #IFCOME to get out of debt.

This couple was in debt for six years and six months. Remember, they had to pay off credit cards, the car, and the student loans before they could start accelerating this mortgage. Combined, it took this couple twelve years and nine months to pay off their debt that was designed to be paid off over thirty years. Remember the two-month time-out we took in the middle to pay off that car repair; that means it took twelve years and eleven months. This is still light years ahead of what your lenders prefer you do.

How much money did this couple save by implementing this strategy? Let's look at some rough numbers.

We shaved seventeen years and one month off their mortgage loan. Let's just round to fifteen years to keep this simple. The mortgage payment was $822.

We'll round down to $800. $800 x 12 = $9600 per year. $9600 x 15 years is $144,000 in mortgage payments.

Would an added $144,000 create an impact on your life? Sure, it's not $144,000 sitting in their bank account, but this is money they will no longer volunteer to pay out to the mortgage company by slow-paying on their loan.

This money is pulled back into their budget to work for them. Could you start to build a retirement with 144,000? Could you use some of that money to help pay for your kids' college? Remember that this couple didn't bring the mortgage payment of $822 back into their budget. When they paid off the loan, they brought back the whole $1580. What could you do with an extra $1580 in your budget every month and NO mortgage or debt?

You could go on a nice, well-earned vacation. When you return, it's time to get down to business. You're going to make this money work for you. Another critical element to be aware of is that this couple was in the plan for twelve years. Were they earning the same incomes at the end of the program as they were when they started?

No, they were earning more. This means it was that much easier to stay on track with this plan to keep the discipline required to be successful.

Now that everything is paid off, this couple lives their designed lifestyle.

If you're going to succeed in the long term, you cannot build real wealth while still paying down debt, especially if you're making payments without seeing any progress. You want to establish your foundational building blocks and construct your financial empire. Know that you cannot reduce debt if you lack a surplus in your budget or don't know if you have a surplus.

I have an animated video showing you the cheapest and most efficient way to get out of debt. To watch this video, scan the QR code below or visit my website: www.financialparachute. com/pages/how-to-pay-down-debt

## Why This Strategy Works

You've seen this strategy before; called the snowball or the avalanche. If you've tried it before without success, I will explain how you can succeed at this process, even if you haven't in the past. This pay-down strategy works when you successfully complete the budget, audit, and monitor steps first. That B.A.M. process is designed to help you find the volunteer money within your budget to accelerate your process, but also carve out unnecessary expenses and develop the discipline to stay on target.

### *Work Smarter, Not Harder*

In the paydown strategy, I was able to show you how effective just $100 would be in your mission to get you out of debt. When I sit down with a couple and show them this strategy, one spouse excitedly says they're going to pick up a lot of overtime to send in $400 every month, to get out of debt sooner. After all, if $100 per month cut your timeline by more than half, what type of impact would $400 create? The reality is, not that much.

When we do the calculations, you would get out of debt sooner by adding more money to your accelerator payment, but you would only save about two years. Granted, that is valuable, but at what cost? We took a thirty-year payment timeline and reduced it down to thirteen years. If changing your accelerator payment from $100 to $400 gets you out of debt sooner by two years, then that means you'll be done in eleven years. That sounds awesome!

But it also means that for eleven years, you worked overtime or a second job to put together enough money to accelerate this plan. For that length of time, you traded time away from your family, your hobbies, or doing the things you enjoy, the things you love, to save just two years of payments.

In my opinion, it's not worth it. With this strategy I've shared with you today, all of these steps are designed to help you retake control of your life, not create a reason to work more. Look, I'm not lazy. I love work. I love feeling productive, I enjoy getting paid to do what I love. I am not saying don't make more, don't earn more. I'm telling you, you can do this with the money you're bringing home today.

Avoid attributing your debt to an inability to work more or earn more. On the flip side, if you can send more than $100 per month, have at it. The more, the better. However, the ability to pay more than $100 must be within your means, not at the cost or sacrifice of something or someone you love.

This entire course is designed for your personal growth and development, not to help you deny yourself things or experiences that enrich your life. This is your opportunity to leave your life behind, which has been molded by years of reacting and layers of arbitrary decisions. Instead, you're now shaping and designing the life you want, the life you deserve; most importantly, it's the life you will create, not anyone else. You have the knowledge and the ability to change your financial future. A better tomorrow is not dependent on getting a raise, working overtime, or winning the lotto.

Your best future is in your hands, and no one can take that away from you.

I need you to understand that it is the discipline that gets you out of debt and the desire to feel what it's like to have financial security. This is not difficult—in fact, this is very simple—but let me be clear: simple does not mean easy. This requires a great deal of willpower. *Simple* means you don't need an MBA or a degree from Harvard to understand this. The greatest ideas in life are the simplest.

## Creating Your Financial Umbrella

Think of financial security as having a trusty umbrella. Just as an umbrella shields you from sudden downpours, a robust financial plan offers protection against life's unexpected financial storms. With a financial umbrella, you're prepared, and you navigate with confidence. Imagine a financial umbrella as your safeguard during financial emergencies, ensuring you and your family remain secure.

What amount of money would make you feel financially at ease? How big should your umbrella be?

Often, when I ask clients how much they need to feel financially secure, the most popular answer is a million dollars. While ambitious, this figure is often plucked from the sky and lacks a concrete strategy for achieving it. Paradoxically, while they aspire for this million, they're also skeptical about ever attaining it. Recognizing this dichotomy is essential because it highlights a deeply ingrained financial insecurity many of us aren't even conscious of.

To address this, let's start by understanding your essential monthly expenses—the bare minimum to keep the household afloat. This figure will shape your financial safety net. Picture this: Your employer announces an impending move overseas, leaving you jobless. With your savings, how long could you carry your expenses without income? When paying your bills, will the mortgage or the student loan weigh heavier on your mind? Essentials like housing, food, utilities, and insurance top the list, while credit cards, medical bills, and unsecured loans can be temporarily sidelined. I envision a debt-free you. However, should you have such debts, remember that in times of financial strain, this financial umbrella prioritizes saving your home and car. Other creditors can wait until you are back on your feet.

Using a hypothetical scenario: If your overall monthly expenses are $6,400, but your essential expenses sum up to $4,000, you now have clarity. In a worst-case scenario, you need $4,000 monthly to operate your household. While neglecting other debts like credit cards or student loans will impact your credit score, immediate survival takes precedence. Course correction can always follow once stability is regained.

Reflect on the transformative impact of having a financial safety net. If you needed $4,000 a month during a financial emergency, how long would it take you to save $12,000 for a three-month cushion? This won't be an overnight achievement, but you now possess three invaluable tools: knowledge of your monthly essentials, a tangible goal, and a road map to achieve it.

Remember the million-dollar benchmark? If you break it down, you might need just $72,000 saved over eighteen months to achieve your financial security. This is a much more attainable goal. So, how much do you genuinely need for financial peace of mind? With structured planning, not only does financial security become achievable, but it's also well within your grasp. This knowledge is transformative.

## Charting the Course

Throughout my career in finance, I have had the privilege of working with clients nearing the age of one hundred. On the other end of the spectrum, I have taught financial literacy to junior high students. The range between eleven and ninety-seven has given me valuable insights into blind spots and many financial regrets. Life's journey is a marathon, not a sprint, marked by distinct phases, each with its own challenges and opportunities. For most people from zero to twenty-one, an adult parent or family member takes care of the significant life necessities and concerns. At this age range, we're sponges, absorbing knowledge without much power to alter our financial paths.

From the ages of twenty-two to forty-two, you are laying down foundations where you test, implement, and sharpen skills for future moves. You want to dive into the job market, experiment with careers, and remember to save more than you spend, especially before family responsibilities kick in. If you're earning $65,000 a year, try living a $55,000 lifestyle. As your earnings rise, maintain that lower-cost standard of living for as long as you can while saving the surplus.

In your **thirties**, beware of the pitfalls of lifestyle inflation. The urge to match or surpass your peers can be tempting, but remember your long-term goals. Focus on investments, in real estate or collaborative ventures that promise returns in the future.

Between the ages of forty-three and sixty-three, you execute plans and leverage your experiences, connections, and relationships more than physical labor, embracing your authentic self. With children soon heading off to college and retirement looming large, this is the time to streamline. Prioritize paying off hefty debts like mortgages. Think about it: eliminating a monthly mortgage frees up significant income, providing more room to turbocharge your savings.

By your **fifties**, the mission should be clear: minimize liabilities. Consider downsizing your living space, especially if the children have moved out. Why maintain a four-bedroom house when something cozier (and cheaper) will do? Reducing your financial footprint now paves the way for more relaxed, enriching golden years. Moreover, your accumulated wisdom over the years is a treasure trove. Consider consultancy or mentoring roles that can be both fulfilling and financially rewarding.

The period after age sixty-four, health permitting can be your most fulfilling years, underscoring the importance of the marathon's later stages, where prudent planning ensures a quality retirement. Financial independence and literacy, starting young and adjusting through life's stages, help navigate the complexities of personal finance. Strategic saving, investing, and spending from early adulthood prepare us for the financial responsibilities of midlife and the freedom and fulfillment of our golden years.

By recognizing the importance of early financial education and strategic planning through life's decades, we can mitigate the "tax events" of financial missteps, achieving both immediate goals and long-term security. The journey from sponge-like learning to wise execution demonstrates that while earning more is beneficial, understanding and managing one's financial course with intelligence and efficiency is paramount.

# Interlude

## Money Will Make
## You Do Things You Don't Want to Do

I said money will make you do things you don't want to do, but really, it's financial insecurity that's pulling the levers. Some stay home and swallow their parents' rules because they don't want to face the real world. Others will get married to escape a home filled with rules. Others will stay in relationships longer than needed because they're not the breadwinner. This doesn't even scratch the surface of crime, theft, money laundering, skimming, gambling, and speculating.

February 2000: I was in downtown Chicago, in the Mid Continental Plaza building, insulated from the winter wind that our great city is known for. I was sitting at my desk when a clicking sound came over the intercom, pausing the sound of dozens of ringing phones. A booming voice said: "Ed, come in to see the Wizzaaard." The intercom clicked, and the orchestra of ringing phones resumed. I got up from my desk and walked toward the corner office. I was on my way to see the "Wizard."

No one looked up; everyone hurriedly handled one call with at least one other caller on hold. The room was filled with desks separated by thin grey partitions only four feet high. The black marble floor running the length of the entire city block acted like an amplifier of the ringing phones. That office encompassed the whole thirty-fourth floor, although only half was in use. The rest of the office was vacant, and that voided space echoed the sound of the phones ringing.

I turned left at Todd's desk; he looked up, raised his eyebrows, and gave an assuring nod. This was the second time in two weeks that I had been in to see the "Wizard."

Pete called himself the wizard—he probably still does. I don't know why, but that's what he called himself. We called him Pete behind his back. To his face, everyone addressed him as Sir. Pete is the owner of this law firm, and he ran it like a tyrant. Pete would walk out of his office shouting at attorneys, berating them, spit flying from his mouth. He ruled with fear. I didn't see this one instance, but I was told he made an attorney run on the treadmill in his suit because Pete didn't like how the attorney handled a matter in court. I believed it because there was a treadmill in the workout room, just twenty feet from the phone pit. There was a Stairmaster, treadmills, weights, and a bathroom with a shower next to the kitchen. This office was high-end. I had no reason to doubt this account, as I had witnessed Pete's rage firsthand on my coworkers. Fortunately, I had never been the recipient of his wrath.

As I entered Pete's office, I had to walk past a wall that created privacy for Pete's desk. Around that wall is his desk, overlooking the Chicago skyline ahead and the boats on Lake Michigan, to the right. I recognized the giant pink artwork that hung on the wall behind Pete; it was the same art I'd seen in his TV commercials, which ran during Bulls games and *Jerry Springer*.

When I took this job, I knew I didn't want it. After researching and applying for clerkships throughout the city, I was left with two options: earn $11 an hour at a corporate law firm, or $14 an hour with unlimited overtime at a consumer bankruptcy law firm. I've never been afraid of work, so I took the bankruptcy clerk position. For reasons stated above, I did not want this job, but money makes you do things you don't want to do.

Pete and I had a conversation about my check when I addressed the fact that none of my overtime was on my paycheck. He acknowledged the discrepancy and said he would fix it. I would need to wait until the following payday for my overtime to be added to my check.

My biggest fear was confirmed, the following paycheck. My overtime hours from the period in question had been applied to my check, but the overtime hours from my current pay period were not. My check was short on overtime pay for the second pay period in a row.

I wanted off this rollercoaster and the only way off was to meet with the Wizard. When I showed Pete my timesheet, I pointed out that my hours were recorded to the hundredth of an hour. I did not understand what more I could do to prevent another "glitch" in my payroll.

Pete looked back at me indifferently, and that's when I knew. He was messing with my money on purpose. He wanted to see if I would fold like the other people he berated in his office. He'd know if I didn't stand up in that moment, he had me. Going forward, Pete would be able to roll over me anytime he wanted. Hell, I was already calling him Sir.

I felt a sudden wave of heat radiate over my head. My fingertips were numb; I couldn't feel my legs. I was brimming with fear and anger. The only part of my body that I could still control were my eyes, and out of the corner of my left eye, I saw John (Pete's assistant) watching Pete and me at a standstill, equally motionless.

I was staring right back at my boss, who flat-out said he wouldn't pay me. What were my options? I told him: "I already have friends; I don't need you to like me, but I need you to respect me. If you don't respect me, no one else out there will." As my eyes pointed with intent, I noticed my right arm was pointing out of his office into the boiler room phone pit.

Pete countered with, "I'm not going to pay it." At that point I had an out-of-body experience; I don't know where this strength came from because I am sure all I felt was fear. I told Pete, "If you don't want to pay me overtime in the future, that's fine, but I've already worked those hours. You made me wait two extra weeks for pay I've already earned, and now you want to do it again. I quit, and you'll pay me what you owe me." I started to walk out of Pete's office, then I turned back and said to him: "You put my check in the mail."

Pete yelled, "Come back here! You don't walk out on me." I turned back three steps around the wall to look at him, and he said: "Get out of my office! Don't you come in here and threaten me." I walked out of his corner office, tilting my head back to keep the pools of water gathering in my eyelids from pouring down my face.

I walked to my desk, grabbed my briefcase, and walked to the elevator as fast as possible. Now, everyone was looking up. I refused to make eye contact because I knew if I did, I would immediately start to cry out of rage and embarrassment.

It was a long way down to the ground floor. I collected myself, walked through the blustering wind, and headed straight to Union Station to catch the train home.

I thought to myself, *Wow, great job, E*. *You are officially unemploye*. That experience aside, I learned a lot during that clerkship. I learned a lot at my next job, which I landed because of my previously acquired experience. Yet, it would take me more than a decade to realize that the financial insecurity I was carrying as a new grad and as someone who had never experienced financial security was driving my decisions even though I knew better.

I believe financial insecurity is what has driven much of our labor force. I believe the world would collectively benefit if that insecurity was wiped out, freeing laborers, technicians, professionals, and experts to work at what they excel in. We would experience unparalleled exponential productivity, creativity, and overall happiness.

> *Limiting Financial Belief:* ***I don't trust banks or credit card companies; they always have hidden fees, traps, and high interest rates.*** – A bit of skepticism is healthy, but it's okay. You are your number one advocate. I aim to help you utilize these financial tools to create your security and ensure lenders don't make a tool out of you.

# Chapter 7

Debt and Debt Instruments

## The Triad: Time, Money, or Credit

With a quarter-century in the bankruptcy and finance industry, I've learned a bit about debt. If you're grappling with debt issues, know this: you can find a resolution, but it's will cost you in either time, money, or credit. Most people seek a solution that preserves their money, maintains their credit, and saves time. If someone offers a solution that promises to protect all three, be aware—it's likely a scam.

If you need to eliminate debt to secure a promotion, finalize a loan, enter a partnership, or secure employment, you can spend your money to pay off the debt, while you negotiate with your creditors to reverse any negative marks on your credit report. In this scenario, you would use your money as leverage. You would save both time and your credit, but not money.

Alternatively, if you lack the funds to address your debt, you can opt to sacrifice your credit. By being unable to pay your creditors genuinely, you essentially starve them out. After several months without payments, your creditors might finally become willing to negotiate a settlement, allowing you to clear your debt for a fraction of the original amount. This approach saves you money—potentially a significant sum—but consumes valuable time and damages your credit entirely. Beyond the time spent positioning your creditors for negotiation, you'll need additional time to recover from the negative marks on your credit report. Your specific situation and goals will determine whether you must sacrifice time, money, or credit.

> *Limiting Financial Belief:* ***I believe using credit cards is irresponsible and reckless.*** – Using credit cards is an essential part of building your credit, which is essential to participating in our economy when shopping for a car, a mortgage, personal loans, insurance rates, and more. Using credit cards to subsidize a lifestyle is dangerous.

## Types of Debt: Credit Cards

Credit cards are tools at their core, and their utility hinges on the user. While banks market them as secure, convenient means to spend, they primarily profit from the high interest rates they offer, pushing consumers to rely on credit cards for everyday expenses. When used properly, credit cards are the key to credit-building. Designed for short-term access to funds, credit cards inherently offer steep interest rates. Thus, undisciplined spending can quickly snowball debt, especially when individuals use cards to sustain their lifestyles beyond their means. In essence, borrowing via credit cards can be a costly affair.

Credit cards are short-term borrowing instruments and were initially marketed to be paid off each month, but they are no longer marketed as such. Credit cards no longer tout their benefits for large purchases or ease of use in an emergency. Instead, credit cards aggressively market their points, miles, and rewards when used on everyday purchases such as at the grocery store and the gas station. The direct and intended goal is to make credit card usage a part of your everyday life. Unsurprisingly, we know these are enticements to become reliant or dependent on credit cards daily. But we also think we're going to outsmart them. We believe we will win the points game and not have a life-altering event during this points-stacking process. Would you accept an invitation for a match from a chess grandmaster with the expectation of being the one who will beat her? We understand, recognize, and revere the skill of the grandmaster. The credit card industry is comprised of financial grandmasters and marketing wizards who have convinced us that we have a really good chance at beating credit cards at their own game.

As of the third quarter of 2022, approximately 83% of adults in the United States have a credit card; this equates to over two hundred million Americans using credit cards for purchase transactions.[10] Of these credit card holders, 56% of all active credit card accounts carried a balance from month to month.[11] This highlights that a significant portion of Americans do not pay off their credit card balances in full each month. Carried-over balances accrue interest and added exposure to additional credit card fees.

Among Americans who carry credit card debt from month to month, more than half have owed their creditors for at least twelve months. Additionally, 40% have had their debt for at least two years, 28% for at least three years, and 19% for at least five years.[12] As a result of purposeful design and accessibility, plus compounding interest, credit cards can be a serious challenge for Americans to pay down or break free from.

Credit cards are short-term debt instruments. Despite the high rates of 10% to 36%[13], credit cards can be paid down efficiently. The paydown timeline is under three years. This relatively short window reduces the overall cost of this high-interest debt. (See the Debt Paydown Strategy in Chapter 6.)

---

[10] "Credit Card Statistics: Debt, Balances, Fees and More [2024]" https://www. themoneymanual.com/credit-card-statistics/.

[11] "2024 Credit Card Debt Statistics" https://www.lendingtree.com/credit-cards/ credit-card-debt-statistics/.

[12] "Poll: 60% who have credit card debt have owed their creditors for at least 12 months" https://www.creditcards.com/statistics/credit-card-debt-poll/.

[13] "What is the highest credit card interest rate?" https://wallethub.com/answers/ cc/highest-credit-card-interest-rate-2140660307/.

Even though directly paying down credit cards is the most efficient and cost-efficient way to pay off credit card debt, it is not the most popular strategy. Consolidation is the most popular method. Superficially, it appears logical, even prudent, to consolidate high-interest credit card debt into a home refinance or HELOC (with considerably lower interest rates), but those debt products are not short-term. A HELOC is a home equity line of credit.

They are long-term debt instruments, so their interest rates are lower because the terms are ten years and above. Rolling credit card debt into a ten-year HELOC or worse, a thirty-year mortgage refinance guarantees lower monthly payments but increases your overall debt to nearly double your debt cost, if not more. Not only does your level of debt double but the root causes are not addressed. As a result, moving credit card debt into a consolidation loan allows more credit card debt to accumulate once again. And the cycle continues.

## Credit Cards Are Not for Emergencies

In the 1980s, American Express sought to persuade Americans to get a credit card. They launched a brilliant and successful marketing campaign, convincing Americans that credit cards were for emergencies. You know exactly what I am saying if you can complete the next phrase. "American Express, never leave home _____ it."

Collectively, as a consumer culture, we embraced the idea that credit cards were for emergencies, believing having one for unexpected car repairs, travel mishaps, or any other unforeseen circumstances was crucial. Here's the truth: your savings are for emergencies, not credit cards. When you encounter an unexpected expense, you should turn to your savings. This approach is how households should operate, but often, they don't.

Regarding unexpected emergencies, 37% of adults cannot afford a $400 emergency.[14] Such an emergency becomes unmanageable for the average American primarily because they are already stretched thin from borrowing. Due to the stacked debt and compounding interest on their debt, many Americans lack the savings to tackle a $400 crisis. Imagine not having savings and being confronted with a $400 emergency car repair. Is borrowing the $400 and accruing interest the best solution? If you choose to borrow, you've just inflated your $400 problem into a more expensive dilemma. In reality, the $400 emergency isn't your primary issue; the real issue is that you don't have a system to create the savings you need. With a savings system in place, when faced with an emergency, you become your own hero instead of depending on someone else.

---

[14] "Report on the Economic Well-Being of U.S. Households in 2022 - May 2023" https://www.federalreserve.gov/publications/2023-economic-well-being-of-us-households-in-2022-expenses.htm

I'll put it bluntly: credit cards sole purpose is for building credit. They're not for points, rewards, or miles. I'll guide you on how to use credit cards as a tool to build credit. By doing so, you'll sidestep the traps and pitfalls of the lending industry. You won't succumb to instant gratification, impulsive spending, or retail therapy. Instead, you'll harness lending and credit to secure your dream home, finance business opportunities, and achieve the financial freedom you deserve. Through strategic use of credit, like loans and credit cards, you can navigate the credit system and demonstrate your creditworthiness.

Recall your high school or college days. If you weren't achieving your desired grades, you sought additional instruction or a tutor. You spent time with someone who had already mastered the subject. Eventually, you recognized that there were specific steps to ensure success rather than taking random and arbitrary measures. This next section is designed for your future credit.

## Tools, Not Traps

Credit cards can be powerful tools, especially for securing online purchases, ensuring financial safety in significant transactions, or building credit. However, the key is to use them wisely. Be the master of this tool, and don't let it master you.

Credit cards are a tool for building credit. To build credit efficiently, you want to keep your credit utilization at 10% or below.

You should not be carrying a balance on your credit cards. If you are, you want to pay down your credit card balances to under 30% of your credit limit. If you cannot pay down the balances to under 30% consider asking for a credit limit increase.

If you are going to ask for an increase, you'll need to ask these three questions first:

1.  Will you need to do a HARD pull on my credit report to approve me for an increase? *(Hard inquiries impact your credit score.)*

2.  Can I request a maximum increase, or must I provide a specific limit amount?

3.  If declined, will you decline my request entirely or will you provide me with a counteroffer? If the credit card company's denial is complete, you may want to start by asking for a 10-20% increase.

If you have a balance on your credit card, your first goal is to reduce your utilization below 30%, which will improve your credit score. The next goal is to reduce your utilization under 10%, which will boost your credit score even more.

## Credit Cards Distort Our Financial Reality

In the pre-credit card era, consumers had a tactile sense of their finances. They knew, almost instinctively, how their spending aligned with their budget. This awareness was invaluable. It was a time when one could only spend what they had, fostering a genuine understanding of one's spending limits and encouraging prudence in the face of tempting purchases.

Enter credit cards. Suddenly, consumers could live beyond their means, using credit to subsidize their lifestyles. These cards masked everyday expenses, keeping them separate from our checking accounts. Credit card payments are typically deferred, giving the illusion of increased spending power. This setup makes it easy for consumers to overspend, and they can fall into this trap month after month. Consequently, people's lifestyles are now defined not by how much they earn but by how much they spend, which are two entirely different concepts.

> *Limiting Financial Belief:* **I feel trapped by paying the minimum payments to my credit cards.** – To break free from this "trap," you must first assess what drew you to use or overuse your credit cards. Being genuine about the cause of the problem and not the problem itself is essential. Then, you can break that cycle and not add to the credit card debt. Lastly, paying down your credit card balances properly will feel liberating versus feeling like you are in an infinite loop.

## How to Use Credit Cards Successfully: Rule of 4%

Before 1982, credit cards were a rarity. If you possessed one, your minimum payment was 5% of the balance. For instance, on a $1,000 balance, you'd be looking at a monthly minimum payment of $50. This system instilled a sense of discipline;

cardholders would only borrow what they could afford to repay, regardless of their credit limit.

Credit card companies researched ways to break that discipline and boost consumer borrowing. A strategic pivot, led by their advisory team, proposed reducing the minimum payment percentage. Grasping the users' adherence to their monthly obligations, they slashed the minimum payment from 5% to 3%, a figure that would continue its descent into the early 2000s. With this change, that $1,000 balance now demanded just a $30 monthly payment.

Suddenly, consumers felt an exhilarating surge in spending potential. They could borrow more, yet their monthly obligations seemed more manageable, even reduced in some instances. This maneuver benefited credit card companies twofold: Consumers were borrowing more, and the lower monthly payments also ensured that card balances lingered for longer, racking up heaps of interest.

Consider this: At a 3% payment rate, it would take over a quarter-century to clear a $1,000 debt. Compare this to the original 5% system, where the same debt would be paid off in about two years. Virtually overnight, credit card companies saw their interest profits skyrocket without even increasing credit limits.

Only when Congress stepped in, advocating for consumers, things began to shift. In 2009, Congress passed legislation requiring credit cards to return minimum payment percentages back to 5%. I wish this is what happened, but it's not the case. Congress imposed a disclosure requirement called the minimum payment warning. Since passing the CARD Act, credit cards have added a minimum payment warning on credit card balance statements. The warning provides the time and the total cost of paying off a balance if only the minimum payment is made without adding to the debt. The warning also illustrates the required minimum payment to pay off the balance in full within three years.

It is undoubtedly a challenge to impose a higher payback rate on debt that has already been accumulated, but at the very least, a higher minimum payment could have been required on new debt incurred in the future. This tightened borrowing requirement would curb borrowing and provide an additional safeguard to credit card borrowers.

This was not the case; consumer advocates largely demanded the 2009 CARD Act to stop the common practice of universal default. That's when credit card companies would offer you a card with an interest rate, but would then change the rate on your credit card balance if you had missed a payment with a creditor who wasn't the credit card. You could have an excellent payment history with your credit card at a 10% interest rate, but if you missed a payment to your car loan or a student loan, the credit card company would bump your interest rate to as high as 29%.

This is just one of the many reasons that I preach that credit cards are a tool for building credit. They are not for emergencies and they are not for points or rewards. If you are carrying a balance on a credit card, I urge you to check your statements. Take your minimum required payment and divide it by the current balance. I'm confident that most of you will discover that your credit card company is asking for a payment in the 2% range. Such a minimum payment will keep you carrying a balance over seventy-five years.

Sending 5% to a credit card company could feel out of reach right now, so I recommend sending 4%. This is the tipping point, and using a 4% payment strategy will eliminate your debt within three years if you're not adding to the balance. Failing to do so can lead you down a perilous path of ever-growing debt, liquidating retirement funds and assets, hefty transfer fees, rising interest rates, and even legal repercussions like lawsuits, wage garnishment, property liens, foreclosure, or repossession. Such missteps will undoubtedly wound your credit.

## Types of Debt: Car Loans

### Three Years Is the Goal. Five Years Is the Max

A car is a liability, not an asset. Liabilities lose their value, and as such, you want to pay them off as quickly as possible and limit your cost of ownership. The car you use daily to get to work and transport your kids to and from school is not a collector's item and will not increase in value. Consider the following when car shopping.

A new car is only new once; a used car is "used" every subsequent day for the rest of its life. New vehicles lose immediate value once driven off the car lot. Save money by buying a car of the same year, but with some miles already on it. Deals for a vehicle of the year appear when the next year's model arrive at the dealerships. Financing can range from preapproved terms that you bring to the dealership or the terms the dealer shops around for you. Your better bet is to arrive with your own preapproval from your local credit union or lender, where you already bank.

Loan terms can range from three years to seven years. Remember that five years from now, your car will not be worth what you agree to pay for it today. The longer you finance something, the more it will cost you. Dealerships focus on getting you "into your car" at a monthly payment they believe you can sustain. What they are getting you into is a loan that will generate commission and financing fees for them but obligate you to pay more finance fees than necessary. When it relates to car loans, the shorter the better.

You can feel a lot of pressure, sitting in a tiny office of a car dealership, waiting for the salesperson to come back with new numbers. Before you sign anything, very simply use the calculator on your phone to multiply the number of months the loan is proposed for by the presented monthly payment.

Compare that staggering number to the purchase price you worked tirelessly to negotiate.

Similar numbers will be disclosed to you when they bring the official financing documents; they'll be disclosed in the TILA, Truth in Lending Act. The TILA is long, should be straightforward, and all the prominent information will be found in three boxes toward the top. That aside, it is a long document and can be intimidating to some. The TILA comes at the very end of what feels like the negotiation battle. By then you are worn down by boredom and stall tactics, and dizzy from all the different numbers thrown around. If you don't like the number calculated on your phone, shut it all down before you even get to the TILA stage of the deal. Just walk away.

**Win the Battle, Lose the War**

In this case, the battle is the sticker price, and the war is the finance room. It's not only important to win the negotiation on the car's purchase price. It is equally important not to give the farm away on financing terms that have been purposely made unclear. Ultimately, for the dealership this is where the money is made. Remember our natural inclination to close an open loop. Despite being offered financial terms that are downright offensive, most will still sign on the dotted line, just looking to end the ordeal of sitting in that tiny office, speaking to multiple people, and having your head spin from all the different packages, terms, and numbers that are put out and moved around. It's like trying to guess right on a numerical three-card monte.

Knowing this is the more common and treacherous landscape, you can choose the alternative. Be the choice architect that designs a space where your likelihood of a better outcome is greatly improved. The first step is to always be aware of your credit report and credit score. Don't wait for your car shopping day to discover what your credit score is. If your credit score is not optimal, you want as much time as possible to take the necessary steps to correct and improve your credit score. The second step is to get preapproval from a lender you already bank with. Having an existing banking relationship will improve your odds of better financing terms. Credit unions typically offer better than market average financing to their existing members. If you are not a member of a local credit union, consider opening a checking or savings account with one.

**Understand the True Cost of Ownership**

The third step is to research the car you want to buy. Understand what it sells for, new and used. A Ford and a Toyota may have the exact purchase price, but the cost to own and operate each vehicle will vary dramatically over the next five years. Research the true cost of owning this vehicle, so you understand the maintenance and driving costs ahead.

The website *E◆mun◆s.com* has an excellent tool that helps you compare the cost of ownership of one model versus another beyond the purchase price and financing. Their calculator tool factors in depreciation, taxes, fuel consumption, maintenance, repairs, and more.

Lastly, make sure you love this car. Despite aiming for a five-year loan or shorter, this is the car you want to drive for the next ten years.

### Turn Your Car Payment into a Retirement Fund Boost

If you didn't develop a savings muscle in your youth, saving money as an adult can be challenging. Fortunately, we become creatures of habit very quickly. Consider your car payment. Once your car is paid in full and that car is officially yours, you've freed up some funds. Here's the idea. I recommend you pretend you still have a car payment once you pay off your loan. It doesn't matter if you're in your twenties, thirties, or even fifties, and you've just cleared your car loan. Now, maintain the discipline of that monthly car payment, but redirect it into your savings. If you've been diligent about your vehicle's maintenance, chances are it's got plenty of roadworthy years left. With the car loan out of the picture, the only occasional expense might include some minor maintenance and repairs.

Imagine turning that $500 monthly car payment into a $500 monthly contribution to your retirement fund. It's a transformative shift, and the best part? You don't need a second job or a pay raise. You're merely reallocating funds you're already accustomed to spending. As we navigate the path of financial growth, let's always keep our eyes on the prize. Our ultimate goal should be to balance preparing for your future self with saving and investing, while honoring yourself in the present moment.

## Types of Debt: Mortgage

### How Homeownership Dreams Become a Nightmare

Owning a home is a dream for many, but it can swiftly become a financial burden. A recent article by *Consumer Reports* revealed that the average American stays in their home for only five to seven years. Driven by career advancement, starting a family, or seeking better schools, homeowners often find themselves in the cycle of perpetually upgrading. In this process, many lose sight of the impact these changes have on creating financial security. What impact does this lifestyle upgrade have on you?

Let me illustrate using a mortgage calculator from Bankrate.com, with certain assumptions in play. Consider a straightforward $150,000 purchase price with a $7,500 down payment (5%). This leaves a principal loan balance of $142,500 at a mortgage interest rate of 7%.

If the homeowner makes regular mortgage payments for seven years and then decides to upgrade, where does that leave their existing mortgage? After seven years, with eighty-four principal and interest payments of $948 each month, the homeowner would have contributed $70,152. Of that total, $10,765.48

would go toward the principal balance, leaving a remaining $131,734.52. The balance, $59,386.52, would be allocated to the interest on the loan.

In other words, after seven years and $70,000 in mortgage payments, less than 10% of the loan gets paid off. Opting to leave this loan to upgrade into a newer or bigger home restarts the mortgage cycle. In this analysis, I assumed a thirty-year, fixed-rate loan at 7%, without any extra payments to expedite the loan clearance.

My hope is that you can see how the temptation to upgrade your home and your lifestyle, if unchecked, could lock you into a lifetime of mortgage payments, enriching the banks and not building you forced savings or equity.

I'm not suggesting you never move or elevate your living standards. But by understanding mortgage structures, you can accumulate equity, save on interest, and carry that wealth to your next home.

### Ways to Reduce Your Mortgage Interest and Overall Cost

There's nothing inherently wrong with a thirty-year fixed-rate mortgage. It often offers first-time home buyers the best chance at maintaining their property. Here are a few strategies to reduce your overall interest payments and build equity faster:

1.  **Annual Extra Payment**: Plan to make one additional mortgage payment every year, perhaps using a tax refund.

This simple step can reduce your loan term by five years, saving you five years' worth of mortgage payments.

2. **Bi-weekly Payments**: Instead of making twelve full payments annually, send half of your monthly mortgage payment every two weeks, resulting in twenty-six half-payments or thirteen full payments yearly. This approach can yield similar savings as the first strategy.

3. **Mimic a Fifteen-Year Mortgage**: Though a fifteen-year mortgage payment isn't double that of a thirty-year, paying an amount closer to the fifteen-year rate, like $1,280, can significantly reduce your loan interest paid. Notify your lender to ensure any extra payments are applied to the principal. If you can't always make the accelerated payment, revert to the standard thirty-year payment for that month.

Strategy number three allows you to be more aggressive on your terms without locking yourself into any commitment. This affords you the opportunity to pull back in the event of a financial emergency or temporary budget tightening.

Accelerating your mortgage paydown can provide a more favorable position when considering home upgrades. The more you pay, the less interest you incur, and the quicker the principal decreases.

## Budget for Repairs, Maintenance, and Upgrades

Instagram, Pinterest, and at least twenty different cable channels are constantly showing us how outdated our appliances, cabinet hardware, backsplash, and kitchen countertops are. Don't get me started on the laundry room that should resemble a French café. Although those home renovation shows keep telling us we "need," delaying some of the upgrades and directing those funds to pay down your mortgage will build significant equity and save you tens of thousands in the long run. These upgrades are beautiful and desirable, but only compound the financial setback when stacked with the home upgrade cycle I previously mentioned.

Many will budget for upgrades but fail to budget for emergencies and repairs. Prioritize creating the financial security you deserve.

Fifteen years will come and go before you know it. Treat your thirty-year mortgage like a fifteen-year mortgage, delay some of those cosmetic upgrades until your home is paid, and then enjoy your savings and the ability to upgrade your rooms as you've always wanted, without the stress of balancing the costs of managing your household and renovations at the same time.

# Chapter 8

## Debt "Solutions"
## That Don't Really Work

Many Americans are behind the eight ball without even realizing it. We often base life's most significant financial decisions on our emotions rather than on concrete data. Here are three straightforward examples:

1. **Recent College Graduates**: Fresh out of college, young people often desire to live in upscale neighborhoods, ideally within walking distance of shops, restaurants, and bars. They crave being at the heart of where the action takes place.

2. **Parents**: They seek homes in good neighborhoods and prioritize proximity to the best schools.

3. **Seniors**: This group typically prefers homes that offer tranquility, away from the hustle and bustle of bars, restaurants, or bustling neighborhoods. As realtors

often say, the first rule in real estate is location, location, location.

## We Make Financial Decisions with Our Emotions

However, consider a typical scenario: A young couple identifies their dream location and starts house hunting. They stumble upon a stunning apartment priced at $2,800 per month. Given their combined monthly income of $5,000, they assume they can comfortably afford it and promptly sign the lease. Unfortunately, by committing to this lease, they've unknowingly opened themselves to potential financial challenges.

I wish this couple had access to the guidelines I provided you in Chapter 6. Unknowingly, this couple has committed more than 50% of their monthly income to their housing, leaving a less-than-adequate amount for transportation, food, insurance, and more. This financial commitment placed them in financial jeopardy and exposed them to financial emergencies. My budget guidelines are designed to help individuals make the most informed decisions to maintain a balanced budget.

## Refinance

### Designed to Improve on Previous Loan Terms

Refinancing is a common strategy consumers use to manage debt. However, it's essential to note that refinancing doesn't "pay off" debt in the truest sense; it merely shifts it. When you refinance, the original loan from one lender is paid off by getting a new loan from another lender. This process often alters the loan's terms, such as its duration, interest rate, and interest type—be it fixed, variable, or interest-only.

Before opting to refinance, pinpoint your primary goal. If minimizing interest is the goal, you might reduce the rate and loan duration. While refinancing offers a means to modify debt, it's crucial to remember that your credit score heavily impacts your refinance options. Always be aware of your credit score before shopping for any lending products.

### Refinancing and Consolidation: The Double-Edged Sword

At its core, refinancing is a tool meant to achieve one primary goal: securing a lower interest rate. Logically, no one would intentionally refinance into a higher rate. The process lets borrowers restructure an existing loan, like a mortgage, to capitalize on falling market rates, thereby reducing the overall cost of borrowing.

Refinancing also allows the borrower to modify the duration of the loan. They might shorten their original loan term to decrease the overall borrowing cost. However, using refinancing as a debt reduction mechanism can be flawed. Genuine debt reduction boils down to two avenues: settling the debt through income, savings, or gifts, or discharging it in bankruptcy. Shuffling debt from one creditor to another while racking up extra fees and interest isn't genuine debt reduction. It's not a debt solution despite it typically providing cash flow relief.

I hear it all too often. Clients will say they refinanced and took money from their mortgage to pay off their credit cards. This tactic is fraught with peril unless there's a concrete strategy to tackle this now-inflated mortgage promptly. Additionally, it's vital to create a plan to address the root causes that led to the initial credit card debt.

Consolidation mirrors this process. It's akin to a child pushing their uneaten food into a small pile on their plate, attempting to give the illusion they've nearly finished. The debt is merely shifted from one lender to another, with added fees and interest.

Many might argue that their consolidation loan, at 11%, is a substantial improvement over their 29% credit card rate. They believe they're making significant savings by cutting the interest on their debt. However, I caution against this line of thinking.

Refinanced mortgages can offer significant financial relief and boost your monthly cash flow. Through refinancing, you could transform $1200 of monthly credit card payments into an additional $264 on to your mortgage. This could translate to a net gain of over $900 additional cash flow per month. While this appears to be a positive net gain, within a refinanced mortgage, you'll pay one and a half times in pure interest for your newly consolidated debt.

That equates to 150% interest. This might go unnoticed when spread over thirty years. Moreover, without addressing the underlying causes of your initial debt, you're more likely to accumulate new credit card debt on top of an inflated mortgage.

## HELOC (Home Equity Loan)

A home equity loan is a type of financing anchored by a homeowner's property. The home's equity determines the loanable amount, which is the difference between its market value and the outstanding mortgage balance. For example, if a house is valued at $300,000, and the homeowner owes $140,000, they have $160,000 in equity. Lenders offer these loans as a way for homeowners to tap into this equity without selling their property.

Despite their popularity, home equity loans are not ideal as a debt reduction tool. Many will take out a home equity loan with an interest rate of 8% or less, to help pay off credit card debt that has an interest rate of 19% or higher.

On paper, it may appear that 8% is better than 19%, but there is a very big difference between a short-term debt, such as a credit card, and an 8% interest rate on a second mortgage.

## Consolidations

Consolidation is the darling of debt relief products offered by lenders. Consumers turn to This "debt reduction" strategy, especially when trying to avoid filing for bankruptcy protection. Consolidation means getting a new loan to settle other debt, like car loans or credit card balances. Understanding that in consolidation, original creditors are paid in full, including the interest they're owed is crucial. Thus, consolidating doesn't save money; it merely centralizes the debt and most certainly includes additional interest. Although consolidation can be a valuable financial tool in certain situations, consolidation is not a universal remedy or cost-saver.

A consolidation firm will suggest bundling all your creditors so you only pay one entity monthly. However, they'll add their fees, they could slightly lower the interest rate on some of the debt and maybe adjust some due dates. The problem isn't paying multiple creditors; it's having the funds to pay all your debts.

Consolidation firms often advise clients to halt payments to creditors to gain negotiation leverage. This tactic will damage your credit score and expose you to added fees, interest, and potential legal exposure. Why pay someone to get you into trouble? You can get into trouble all on your own and for free. You don't need a broker or a lawyer to negotiate for you. As one of the two parties in the debt agreement (the other being the lender), you have all the power you need to negotiate.

**The Hidden Costs of Debt "Solutions"**

Whenever I hear those radio ads, they shout at me. They proclaim that Americans can access millions of dollars in home equity and should seize this golden opportunity. The pitch continues: pay off those credit cards, medical bills, and student loans. Buy your dream boat or take that well-deserved vacation.

Such advertisements genuinely infuriate me. Using borrowed money to pay down debt merely moves the debt around and adds more interest to the problem. Anyone possessing equity in their home should recognize it as a forced savings, and that accumulated value in that property should be available for retirement. The ideal scenario is owning a fully paid-off house during retirement, not one burdened with a mortgage and multiple equity loans.

Moreover, if someone is grappling with credit card debt, medical bills, or student loans, it's not wise to create new debt or leverage their home for luxuries like a boat or vacation.

Loans and financial products are tools offered by lenders. These are instruments ordinary people can utilize to purchase a home or vehicle. They shouldn't be exploited to perpetually cycle debt from one form into another, like transferring a credit card balance to an equity loan.

Remember, lenders are in the business of lending and gaining profit. While they aren't necessarily malevolent, their solutions, which offer monthly cash flow relief, most certainly lead consumers deeper into debt. Financial products are tools for you to use. Don't let yourself become the instrument through which lenders amass their fortunes.

I also have issues with debt management plans. If you're finding it difficult to pay your creditors monthly, the problem isn't the number of creditors you have; it's a cash flow issue.

Using a debt management plan, adds thousands of dollars in service fees to your debt. These high fees are typically buried in your "savings." Moreover, this strategy damages your credit score, and the repercussions of a lowered score will prove costly in the long run.

It's understandable for consumers to explore popular debt solutions in the market to avoid bankruptcy. While it's healthy to be wary of bankruptcy, making moves that compound financial issues is counterproductive. Debt management plans expose you to added risk with your creditors when they propose you stop paying the creditor to leverage them into a negotiable position. This trashes your credit history and exposes you to collections, lawsuits, and more.

Each of these "solutions" comes with its own set of repercussions, either financially or in terms of your credit score. Awareness is key before committing to any of these options. There is no magic pill for debt.

## Credit Repair

The most popular debt solutions have more "cons" than "pros" engineered into them. Adding insult to injury, the number one proposed solution to fixing your credit report after you fall financially is just a façade itself.

## The Illusion of Credit Repair

The credit repair industry, worth billions of dollars, thrives on a fallacy. A credit report is a historical document, chronicling your past debt payments and credit management practices. Let me explain how a credit report functions.

Think back to high school. What could you do If you received a B, C, or D in a class but aimed for an A? Your sole option was to put in more effort going forward and strive to elevate your grade.

If you finished a semester with a grade point average (GPA) that disappointed you, your only recourse was to put in more effort the following semester, aiming for a higher GPA to enhance your overall average.

Whether high school was a recent experience or a distant memory, reflect on this: Was there an option for "report card repair?" Could you approach a business, promising to remove all negative grades from your report card and miraculously boost your GPA? Of course not. Such a service didn't exist.

The notion of credit repair is similarly flawed. Businesses making grandiose promises about skyrocketing your credit score usually rely on a single tactic: they dispute negative or derogatory information on your credit report until it's removed or until you grow weary of their monthly fee for ongoing disputes.

Removing negative items could only be temporary, causing your credit score to shoot up and pull back like a rubber band. The most common "solution" these firms propose is for you to continue to paying a monthly fee, so the disputing can continue. This is not removal but suppression, and it gets expensive.

Much like in high school, if you aspire to improve your credit score, the genuine approach is to manage your finances more diligently in the future, ensuring that your efforts are accurately reflected in your credit report.

If there are errors on your credit report that have a negative impact on your score, you can dispute them yourself at no cost and achieve the same results.

**The Expensive Trap of Credit Repair**

Here is the process.

1. A credit repair shop will dispute a reported debt; then the creditor has thirty days to respond. If the creditor is too busy to respond within thirty days, the bureaus will take the debt off your credit report. *This creates an artificial and temporary boost in your credit score.*

2. Forty-five days, or sixty days, into the future, once the creditor does have the time to get caught up with these disputes, they confirm the debt and report it as accurate on your credit report. *The debt reappears, bringing down your credit score once again.*

3. Credit repair shops will charge monthly fees to keep the dispute juggling act going. If they keep disputing and you keep paying, your score will remain artificially high. As soon as they stop disputing, your score will drop.

4. Beware of credit repair companies that charge upfront fees for similar services. This is not how to "rebuild" your credit for long-lasting success. I call this juggling act *suppression*, and I want you to understand the difference between suppression and deletion.

5. Suppression is temporary and expensive. It only lasts if you pay the monthly fees to the credit repair company.

6. Deletion is when something is permanently removed and it never comes back. You aim to delete all inaccurate information from your credit report and build a solid credit history.

## Beware of "No Payments Until…"

Those flashy furniture store commercials blaring "No payments or interest until the next Memorial Day!" might tempt you. But here's the hidden truth: if, when that next Memorial Day rolls around, you haven't paid off your furniture purchase, expect to see a year's worth of interest slapped onto your balance faster than you can say "fine print." Offers that defer payments might sound great, but it's essential to sift through the surface and understand the potential pitfalls.

Taking a no-interest offer when you have all the money to purchase your item outright is savvy and frees up cash flow for a period, so you can make that money work for you. Taking a no-interest offer out of necessity or desperation is the first sign that this is not a scenario where you are likely to win. As your decision architect, you want to choose an option with better odds for success.

## Stay Away from Debt Multipliers

These don't help you; they help the lender. If any of the above appeal to you, let this be your check-engine light. You are in the high-stress, high-risk zone. This is my observation, not a criticism. I've been there myself.

### Death of Loan Sharks

The rampant availability and access to payday and short-term loans have wiped out the market for loan sharks. Why borrow from someone who can hurt you if you don't pay back on time, when you can borrow without the risk of physical injury? The short-term loan options come with interest rates as high as 400%. When people borrowed money from loan sharks, they knew the rates were high, the stakes were higher, and that they were not on the winning end of a transaction. Short-term lenders market themselves as providing valuable services to their communities. Try hearing that sales pitch from a loan shark. Now, borrowers get confused and interpret high-interest short-term loans as convenient or even helpful.

Standard practices for short-term lenders are to offer loans under $1,000 due in one week. The week maturity date is essential because it allows the lender to "reassure" the borrower that they are not making a long-term commitment regardless of the astronomical interest rate. The borrower fails to see clearly that this weekly loan will grow so quickly, they will need to renew the same loan about the following week. In essence, the borrower has locked themselves into a weekly borrowing cycle. Many lenders require electronic access to the borrower's checking account.

These types of loans are so predatory in nature that in 2006, Congress enacted the Military Lending Act (MLA), which targeted many of the standard practices of short-term lending, such as payday loans and even title loans.

Title loans are high-interest rate loans that use a vehicle's title as collateral. Due to the importance of national security, Congress recognized the vulnerability among young military members, who may be managing their finances independently for the first time. Should a service member fall into enough debt, they may be targeted as vulnerable to compromise.

The MLA places a cap of 36% interest on any loan offered to service members. Additionally, title loans offered to military members or immediate family cannot require a car title to be signed over as collateral.

The regulatory protections took a long time to develop and are essential in protecting the great men and women of our military. I believe that recognition of these exorbitant and predatory lending practices should be enough to curb that amount that can be charged to any American, regardless of their service status.

As of this writing, twelve states go beyond the MLA and ban payday lenders entirely, primarily because of the astronomical interest rates charged to consumers.

> *Limiting Financial Belief:* ***I don't understand credit reports and scores. I don't know much about them.*** Understanding your credit score is not complex, and once you are familiar with the moving parts, you can alter how you navigate and interact with everything that impacts your credit score, both positively and negatively.

# Chapter 9

---

# Credit

## Credit Report

### What Is a Credit Report?

A credit report is a report card of how you have utilized lending products in the last seven to ten years. Have you borrowed responsibly? Have you overborrowed? Have you paid back your lenders on time and as scheduled? Paying late, defaulting, and over-borrowing will bring down your creditworthiness.

A credit report represents your creditworthiness on paper. It is in your best financial interest to understand the information in your report, how it gets there, and if the information is accurate.

There are five major components of a credit report. I am going to break these down for you.

### Payment history: 35%

Paying your creditors on time is a significant part of your credit score.

## Balances based on credit limits (utilization rate): 30%

You want to make sure your credit limits are being reported accurately.

## Age of your accounts: 15%

The average age of your credit impacts your score; the older, the better.

## Credit type (credit mix): 10%

Examples include home, car, credit cards, and gas cards.

## Inquiries: 10%

Who is pulling your credit? Are you applying for many loans?

How well you manage and pay your accounts is reflected on your credit report, the way a report card shows how well you did on your assignments, homework, and tests. A credit report shows future creditors and potential lenders what kind of a credit "student" you are. By reviewing your credit report, the potential lender will learn if you have consistently paid your creditors on time. Potential lenders want to know if you can successfully manage more than one type of debt: like a mortgage, a car loan, and a credit card.

The potential lender will be able to see how long you've been in the credit/borrowing system and see what your track history has been. For this reason, it is so important to monitor your credit report closely and regularly. You want it to be 100% accurate.

## Why It Matters

*Limiting Financial Belief: I feel powerless when it comes to my credit score, because I don't know much about it.*

Both a credit report and credit score represent your ability to manage and pay your house, car, credit cards, and loans on time. A potential lender is interested in your credit history to find the answer to just two questions:

1. Should they lend you money?

2. At which interest rate?

For many, credit feels like a game, and as a result, they don't want to play or engage at all with their credit. I understand that fully. It is a game, and it's important that you not only know the rules but also make them work for you. Failing to manage your credit will limit your access, increase your cost of living, and restrict your opportunities, in the short and long term.

### Access

Your credit score can impact your access to housing, career advancement, affordable insurance, utilities, and favorable lending rates.

### Cost and Opportunity

Maintaining clean and accurate credit makes everything in life more expensive and exponentially more challenging. As listed above, consequences include missing out on a renting opportunity, paying hundreds of thousands more on a higher rate mortgage, getting passed on for a promotion, paying more for substandard insurance coverage. The ultra wealthy borrow just as much if not more than the lower class, but they borrow at rates between 1% to 3%, using their assets as collateral. The middle and lower classes borrow at 29% using credit cards. One of these borrowing groups is going to do better over time.

## How to Keep Your Credit Report Accurate

Monitor your credit report regularly. A website such as creditkarma.com does not charge for access to your credit report, and it does not ask for your bank account information, just in case.

This website does support its operations by placing ads in front of likely candidates. You are not required to click on any of those ads.

For a free look at your credit report, you can go to www. annualcreditreport.com. This is a government-sponsored webpage that grants you access to one free credit report per year from each of the top three credit bureaus. You'll want to download the credit report immediately, as this website does not give you back-and-forth access to your report. This is why I call it a free look. With a commercial website like creditkarma. com, you can create an account, which gives you the ability to visit and track your reports as you wish.

When you discover information that is inaccurate, false, or not your information, you want to dispute the information directly with the bureau. I recommend you submit your dispute in writing and include a return receipt with your dispute. This way you can keep a record of when your dispute was received. The bureau is required to respond within thirty days of receiving your letter.

## Credit Score

### What Is a Credit Score?

I want you to think of your credit score as your GPA. I showed you how a credit report is like your high school report card. Your credit score is the numerical equivalent of your grades for paying your debts and managing your credit.

If a potential lender cannot access your credit report to read your credit history, but they can access your credit score, then they can get a pretty accurate sense of what your credit management is like.

Scores range from 350 to 850. Errors and negative marks on your credit report will bring down your overall credit score. Each of the major credit bureaus calculates their own credit score for you. The most well-known credit scores is the FICO score.

Your credit report and credit score will impact your ability to access financing for your home, a car, a loan, and more. Keeping your credit score as high as possible is recommended, to give you access to borrowing at lower and preferred interest rates.

## How to Be Successful

I have compiled a list of the items that will significantly impact your credit score and items that aren't worth pursuing because of the minimal impact that such corrections will have.

## What Doesn't Affect Your Credit Score?

1. Your education level or background

2. The number of years you've lived in a single location or your current location

3. Your salary

4. Payments less than thirty days late do not impact your score, nor are they reported to the credit bureaus.

5. Late payments to your utilities do not impact your score unless they are in collections.

6. Bounced checks do not impact your score unless they are in collections.

7. Rent payments, late or current, do not impact your score unless you are evicted.

8. Historically, rent has contributed to a person's credit history. As of this writing, there are growing instances where you can have your rent payment history reported and in-kind build up your on-time payment history.

While this practice has not been fully adopted by all credit bureaus and landlords, be sure to inquire, as this is a great on-ramp to building credit.

9. Child support or alimony payments do not impact your score, as long as you pay on time.

10. Your race, religion, nationality, gender, or marital status

11. Personal inquiries to your own credit report or inquiries by an employer

**What Does Impact Your Credit Score?**

Everything that does appear on your credit report can be reported for up to seven years. This includes lawsuits, judgments, and foreclosures.

Bankruptcy can remain on your credit report for between seven to ten years. Inquiries appear for two years. Liens against property are reported for up to seven years from the date of satisfaction. Managing your credit report information properly will improve your credit score.

> *Limiting Financial Belief:* ***If I file bankruptcy, I will lose my car or they'll take my house away.*** An adequately prepared bankruptcy is designed to help you protect the property you wish to keep and give you the maximum relief from your creditors while protecting your interests.

# Chapter 10

————⌃————

# Bankruptcy

## How Bankruptcy Works

The two best-known bankruptcy chapters are for consumers: Chapter 7 and Chapter 13.

Chapter 7, often referred to as *liqui*ation bankruptcy, is intended for individuals who lack the means to pay off their current debts. It allows for the erasure of most debts, promising a fresh start. In Chapter 7, debtors must list all debts and assets. A bankruptcy trustee is appointed to oversee the case, evaluating assets (like property and cars) to determine if any property can be sold to repay debts. However, there are exemptions to protect the consumer. Certain personal assets, such as basic household items, a modest car, and some work tools, are exempt from sale. The specifics vary by state.

Chapter 13, known as *reorganization bankruptcy*, is better suited for individuals with regular income who can repay at least a portion of their debts. Debtors can propose a repayment plan to the court, independently or with an attorney. This payment plan outlines how they will repay their debts (or a portion thereof) over time, typically between three to five years. The monthly payment amount depends on the debtor's income, expenses, and types of debt.

Other types of bankruptcy exist. Chapter 9 bankruptcy is for municipalities such as cities, towns, and villages. Chapter 11 bankruptcy is for large corporations. Chapter 12 bankruptcy is a lot like Chapter 13 but is reserved exclusively for farmers.

## Qualifying for Bankruptcy

Both Chapter 7 and Chapter 13 are tools federal law provides to assist individuals facing financial hardships. The choice between the two largely depends on the individual's specific situation. I often hear clients say, "I want to file for this chapter of bankruptcy," or "I would never file for that chapter." It's important to understand that the choice of bankruptcy is predominantly determined by the financial situation one presents.

Petitioners disclose their income, expenses, assets, and liabilities in the bankruptcy application. The decision of which bankruptcy to file is predetermined based on their cash flow, assets, and earnings. If a person is working with an attorney, the attorney will perform an analysis like that of the court-appointed trustee. This analysis determines the most appropriate bankruptcy chapter.

Not everyone qualifies for Chapter 7. To be eligible, your income must be below a certain level, as determined by a means test. This test compares your income to the median income in your state. For Chapter 13, the petitioner must have a regular income. Additionally, their unsecured and secured debts must fall below certain limits.

## Bankruptcy Advantages and Disadvantages

In a Chapter 7 bankruptcy, an individual can discharge debts. This includes medical bills, credit card balances, and debts from a failed business - also, loans on property they no longer wish to keep. In a Chapter 13 bankruptcy, an individual can retain all assets. This includes saving their home from foreclosure. It can even stop a repossession or wage garnishment. In both types of bankruptcy, the debtor receives protection from creditors. And relief from debts that could otherwise burden them for decades. Filing for bankruptcy is not ideal; and can bring a social stigma associated with financial trouble. Another significant downside is that the "fresh start" promised in bankruptcy is not automatic.

A Chapter 7 bankruptcy remains on a credit report for ten years, while a Chapter 13 bankruptcy stays on for seven years. However, a debtor can still obtain loans and rebuild credit post-bankruptcy. This "fresh start" depends more on credit management than the actual filing. If creditors properly report discharged debts as a zero balance, a fresh start is well underway. However, creditors often do not update or clear negative information from a credit report. This means a credit report may still show outstanding debts after bankruptcy. It is essential to understand that neither improvement nor maintenance of your credit is included in a bankruptcy filing. Once a bankruptcy is discharged, the credit rebuilding process for the petitioner begins.

> *Limiting Financial Belief:* **Bankruptcy will ruin my credit forever.** – In some instances, your credit can recover faster when coming out of bankruptcy than limping along, swimming upstream, and trying to get out of debt.

## When Should You Investigate Your Bankruptcy Options? The Three-Year Rule

In Chapter 6 of this book, I explain how to reclaim control of your household budget by using the B.A.M. strategy. Reclaiming that control is crucial to have success with any version of the snowball method. If you earnestly follow my strategies plus the snowball and cannot map a way out of debt in three years or less, then it's time to investigate your bankruptcy options.

In my career, I have reviewed thousands of credit reports. And almost like reading the tree rings on a log, I can pinpoint with forensic-like precision all the previous failed attempts to get out of debt and avoid bankruptcy. It most commonly looks like opening more credit cards, then a consolidation loan or a mortgage refinance, followed by more credit cards, a new loan, and the debt cycle continues. In between are the multiple collections and the lawsuits throughout. Every step along the way adds to your stress and to your debt.

It would be one thing if it were only debt accumulation. Still bankruptcy avoidance tactics also include rounds and rounds of wiping out personal safety nets via liquidating assets, cashing out life policies, and even draining retirement accounts prematurely.

I have seen financial trauma drag out for more than a decade. That is a long time to struggle. What is more disheartening is the future void and long-term impact that the liquidation of those safety nets creates.

> *Limiting Financial Belief: **I am embarrassed because I carry credit card debt.*** – Rule number 1 -Never identify your self-worth based on how much you have or don't have. Rule number 2 -The rich don't give A.F. about having debt. See rule number 1. Rule number 3 -There's a better, more cost-effective way.

Every solution has a price, and that price has to make sense. Paying $9,000 in fees to consolidate $30,000 of debt and ruin your credit does not make sense. Paying $2,000 to wipe out $7,000 in credit card debt through bankruptcy doesn't make sense either. Every situation has intricate considerations, but making the problem bigger and last longer should never be a part of the outcome.

This is why the decisions that challenge our egos, pride, and sense of self are so difficult on their surface. But if we remove our ego, pride, and identity and do the math, the path to an efficient solution reveals itself much more quickly.

> *Limiting Financial Belief:* **I'm not rich, and building a retirement account takes a lot of money.** - Starting with any money is how is better than delaying. The key is to start today; taking action is what offsets starting with a small amount.

# Chapter 11

## Investing

### Acquire Assets over Liabilities

The sole purpose of keeping your expenses lean from the beginning is to build financial security: first by saving, then by investing. Ultimately, you want to be a serious investor. Investing in an income-generating asset is how you will become financially independent. Suppose you want to vacation, remodel your home, buy a new car, or pay off student loans. Your income-generating assets should pay for these, not your nine-to-five employment income.

The financially savvy operate using a simple model: spend less than you earn, save the difference, and invest in assets. These assets range from stocks and bonds to real estate or value-appreciating collectibles. Want to finance a house, afford annual vacations, support your child's education, or secure a comfortable retirement? While many try to juggle these dreams on a single income, investing in assets that churn out regular cash flow is the way to affluence.

This embodies the concept of multiple streams of income. If one asset underperforms, you have others to fall back on, plus your primary income. Life happens to all of us. What if you were to work fewer hours due to illness or injury? Your assets could ensure you don't miss a beat financially.

The next time you're on vacation, standing at a hotel's check-in counter, glance at your fellow guests. Ever wonder who's paying for their vacation? Is this getaway financed with borrowed money? Or is this merely one of several leisure trips, all bankrolled by their assets? Maybe they're even scouting investment opportunities as they unwind.

Consider an NFL player's trajectory. Their career, while lucrative, is fleeting, averaging around eight years. The same principle applies to us, albeit on a more modest scale. We, too, have a professional shelf life.

It's universally understood that professional athletes must invest wisely for list post-retirement since they have a limited earning window. Why, then, do we seldom apply this logic to ourselves?

For a more comfortable, secure, and flexible life, a single income source won't suffice. You need assets that generate income, assets that work for you even as you sleep.

*Limiting Financial Belief:* ***I feel overwhelmed by the complexity or the size of the retirement goal numbers.*** – One million dollars is too much to fathom without a plan. Let me show you your retirement number and how your journey will differ from what you expect.

## Don't Let the Stock Market Intimidate You

Many people shy away from investing because they perceive it as overly complex. They are not entirely wrong; investing can indeed be complex, and there are numerous ways to go awry. However, investing doesn't have to be complicated, and you can mitigate your risk of loss.

I often explain investing to my junior high students by comparing it to picking a winning horse at a racetrack. If you pick the right horse, the feeling is exhilarating. Choose wrongly, and you might swear off betting at racetracks altogether. Similarly, the investment market is teeming with brokers and advisors who claim they can help you pick the right "horse." They will tout their track record of picking winners and charge a percentage of your account for their services.

For our lesson, I ask my students to overlook that betting on horses is gambling, whereas investing is not. Let's say a typical day at the racetrack has twelve races. This means there are twelve winners, twelve second-place finishers, and twelve third-place finishers. How can one possibly predict the outcome accurately? Yes, handicapping is indeed complicated.

Here's where the lesson pivots: even with all these races, the racetrack consistently makes money, not just the jockeys or horse owners. Instead of betting on a single horse, why not consider the racetrack as the day's guaranteed winner? This is because, the racetrack profits from the day's operations despite the individual winners and losers. Similarly, the horses in our analogy represent publicly traded companies, and the racetrack represents an entire index, such as the S&P 500, Nasdaq, or the Dow Jones Industrial Average.

My students are often surprised to learn that one can invest in an entire index. With this newfound knowledge, they are still cautious about the potential to lose money.

I reassure them: you don't need to be an expert in selling hamburgers to profit from McDonald's success, nor must you understand marketing, shipping, or technology to benefit from the operations of Walmart, Amazon, and Microsoft. Let those who excel at making money do so, while you invest in an index comprised of solid businesses. Whether you are a student, parent, doctor, dancer, or grandparent, these companies strive for growth and success.

You will continue your education, earn degrees, and pursue careers that may not relate to finance. Therefore, don't divert mental energy and time from your chosen field to unravel the complexities of investing. This is a common stumbling block. Many are experts in plumbing, mechanics, bioengineering, or even professional basketball, yet they know little about stocks or the market. Thinking they need to hire an advisor or a broker, they overlook a more straightforward approach: investing in an index.

Life is simpler when you realize that Fortune 500 companies employ teams of lawyers, accountants, and PhDs, all working toward the success of their companies. This is the first benefit to investors. More importantly, you don't need to pick the perfect company. By investing in the broader index, which is made up of both winners and lesser performers, you let the index do the heavy lifting. When a company underperforms and falls below specific criteria, the index replaces it with stronger, more successful companies, akin to a racetrack that retains only the best horses in its stables.

## My Humble Theory on Investing

A while back, a technician came to my home to do some work. He was a young guy, and during our conversation about work, he asked me about investing. I gave him a brief overview of how to get started while minimizing risk and exposure. He became excited and asked, "Okay, when do I get that money? When can I use it?"

That's when it hit me: he wasn't ready to invest successfully because he was in survival mode. Despite how simple and fundamental the basics of investing for your future can be, if you are counting on spending the money you invest, you will find it very hard to get motivated to invest.

A retirement account is a lot like a forest or a field filled with mature trees. Your goal is to have an endless supply of large, strong trees that will provide shade and protection for you and your family during your retirement. Not many people can afford a fully mature tree, especially in retirement. You want to buy the trees when they are just seedlings or saplings, which is much more affordable.

To accomplish this goal, you invest by buying seedlings when the market is low. You buy saplings when the market is higher, but you never stop buying because prices fluctuate. Instead, when prices drop, you should rush to buy as many seedlings as possible because they are much cheaper than saplings. When prices increase, and only saplings are available on the market, buy more to fill your land, as saplings are still more affordable than fully mature trees.

You'll look out over your field or backyard of saplings and might question yourself, especially during slow growth periods. There will be years when it seems like your trees have frozen in time or shrunk, though we know that's impossible. No one will envy you. Many of your peers will judge you, wondering why you invested so much in that barren-looking field instead of partying more, vacationing more, or spending your money on shiny objects as they do.

Have you ever questioned if a tree would mature? We know that rain or shine, a small tree will eventually grow into a big tree. Life will continue around it—graduations, weddings, jobs, and promotions. The trees grow undisturbed by these life events. They grow independently while you're at work and while you sleep. They also drop seeds of their own, helping your modest forest expand. They will be there when you are ready to enjoy the shade under the trees you've planted.

People will walk by and admire the strong, mature trees you have. They'll say, "Man, she's so lucky." You'll remember how no one envied you when you were making sacrifices. In this analogy, seedlings and saplings represent stocks. You want to buy as many stocks as possible at the lowest prices available over time so that they mature with compound growth for your retirement.

## Step 1. Recognize the Game.

> *Limiting Financial Belief:* ***I distrust advisors, investment firms, and fast talkers.*** - This is fair, but you can do a lot on your own. Start by reading just one financial article a day. You'll understand ten times as much in six months as you did on day one. When you educate yourself, no one can talk down to you.

The markets are complex, and many people offer ways to grow your money quickly. You'll see this with day-trading platforms, "experts," and stock pickers. Remember, you're in the tree game and want to buy only seedlings and saplings. The promise of a fast-growing tree is shaky at best.

**Step 2. Recognize Your Weaknesses, Strengths, and Comfort Level.**

I see "experts" all over social media boasting about how they turned $1,000 into $10,000. If you've seen these claims and felt your heart rate increase, it's an indicator that you're eager for more money but lack the necessary security. This is dangerous. Don't get sucked in. Conduct a self-assessment. Are you impulsive or indecisive? Does risk paralyze you, or do you tend to seek out long shots and go all-in? Being aware of your personal tendencies will help you remain focused on your long-term goals when market conditions shift.

Every time you invest in a seedling or a sapling, you will have feelings afterward. They may be exhilaration or remorseful. The most important feelings to document, literally write down, are the feelings you were experiencing at the time of your investment. Did you feel rushed, were you afraid of missing out, were you too excited, did you second-guess for too long? Always make your big decisions from a place of certainty and calm. Never make a big decision under duress or stress.

The biggest money managers in the world put a greater emphasis on not losing money than they do on gaining more money. The unskilled investor is willing to take on great levels of risk for the promise of a large or quick gain. It is clear that one strategy is sounder than the other.

**Step 3. Ignore the Market Noise.**

Don't follow the financial news with the intent of making immediate decisions. Consider this: if there was twenty-four-hour news coverage about how trees grow or sway in the wind, would you watch it? Constant market data, analysis, and speculation can confuse investors. Whether or not you monitor the financial news, you know your seedlings will grow to maturity. Moreover, you don't have enough insider information or the computational power to time the market effectively. Leave that to the hedge funds and major brokerages.

**Step 4. Never Stop Buying.**

Don't wait and save up your money waiting for the perfect time to invest. We've already discussed the futility of trying to time the market. Instead, buy your stocks/shares incrementally. For example, instead of investing $5,000 all at once, invest $500 each month for ten months. This strategy, known as *dollar-cost averaging*, helps balance out your purchase price over time. Even in times of high market prices, continue to buy your seedlings. You're in this for the long haul.

Time is your most valuable investment asset. If you plant two saplings side by side, five years apart, the latter one will never catch up to the first, no matter how much better you care for it.

You can't make up for lost time. So, plant your seedlings and saplings today, and make the most of your time asset.

## Investing in the Stock Market Efficiently

You want to dollar-cost average your money into index funds or low-cost ETFs.

Examples include Vanguard S&P 500 ETF (VOO) and SPDR S&P 500 ETF Trust (SPY).

If this feels oversimplified and unsophisticated, it is. Too many people make too much money off of novice investors by overcomplicating this simple process.

You can invest in these types of funds inside your 401(k), an IRA, a Roth IRA, or independently of these accounts.

# Chapter 12

—⌒—

# Retirement Planning

Retirement can be incredibly intimidating or overwhelming for many. For everyone else, it doesn't even register because they are younger than thirty-five and feel like retirement is a million years away. Retirement will not be overwhelming if you can put yourself in the shoes of the future, in order to apply some necessary perspective. 1. Know how to measure true wealth. 2. Begin to shrink your financial footprint; the earlier, the better. 3. Adopt a strategy for your retirement savings.

## How to Measure True Wealth

Many people feel wealthy because they wear nice clothes and have expensive things. Many more people look wealthy because they borrow money to live a fancy lifestyle, but they lack savings and security.

True wealth is not a universal benchmark, like five million or ten million dollars. True wealth is personal to you. The amount of money you need to be and feel financially secure could dramatically differ from the amount I need. Therefore, having three million dollars in a retirement account could be sufficient for me and not remotely close for you. How do you know what that magic number is? How do you measure true wealth?

True wealth is the ability to stop working and maintain the lifestyle you want to live without returning to work. If you were to stop working today, how long could you afford your current lifestyle? For some, it might be an impressive six years; for others, a mere three weeks; and unfortunately, for a significant number, not a single day due to overwhelming debt.

Here's a simple exercise: Calculate your monthly lifestyle expenses, factoring in housing, utilities, food, transportation, insurance, and a ballpark figure for medical costs. Now, annualize this number by multiplying it by twelve. Your aim is to amass a sum that can annually pay you this amount, without dwindling the principal amount. As your savings or investments accrue interest, ensure that your withdrawals don't outpace its growth.

## Your Financial Parachute

Using the B.A.M. process detailed in Chapter 6, you will have created a disciplined approach to paying down your debt and building a savings simultaneously. Once you surpass paying off your home in the pay-down process, you can accelerate your savings. This is when you shift gears and transform your financial umbrella into a financial parachute.

For the first fifteen years of my career, the advice I would give at lectures, in the classroom, and online was all the same. Save to build your financial umbrella; save a minimum of six months of your monthly necessity expenses to protect yourself. It wasn't until I read an interview with Ray Dalio where he explained how he recommended to his multimillionaire families to save a minimum of six years of annual expenses. I recognize Ray's clients are on a completely different scale, but this still blew my mind. The rationale for saving between six to seven years' annual expenses is that if the markets slide or crash, his clients are not pressured into selling valuable assets at distressed prices to stay afloat. This cushion affords his clients the ability to hold assets and even acquire more stock when the markets go down versus cashing out in desperation, along with the rest of the herd.

I don't know if Mr. Dalio has a name for the six-year emergency fund, but I call it a financial parachute. If the floor fell out from under our feet, we would desperately need a parachute. In Chapter 6, I provide you with the steps for building your financial umbrella. Building your financial parachute is just the next level. Once you've paid off your car, credit cards, student loans, and mortgage early, you can stack your savings much quicker, building that essential security.

It all starts with naming a process and then mapping out a plan. You will take control of your budget and implement a process to build your financial umbrella. As you gain wisdom and experience, this umbrella will evolve—much like yourself—into a financial parachute. All of this leads to manageable guided stewardship that you own and control leading up to your retirement.

## Shrink Your Footprint

Financial experts often suggest a simple benchmark: set aside ten times your annual income for retirement. Let's break this down. If you earn $50,000 annually, the formula recommends saving $500,000 for retirement. The idea is that this sum, with a conservative 4% return, can offer you a steady monthly income during your golden years.

Just over 50% of Americans earn $75,000 or less annually.[15] Here's the catch: how many individuals genuinely live within their means? A 2023 survey reports that 61% of Americans carry credit card debt.[16] This debt primarily stems from spending more than one earns. If the majority spent within their means, debt wouldn't be such a widespread issue.

---

[15] "Credit Card Debt: 1 in 4 Americans Fall Deeper Into Debt Each Month (2023 Data)" https://listwithclever.com/research/average-american-credit-card-debt-2023/.

[16] "Credit Card Debt: 1 in 4 Americans Fall Deeper Into Debt Each Month (2023 Data)" https://listwithclever.com/research/average-american-credit-card-debt-2023/.

Relying solely on this formula may mislead you. It's essential to create a financial plan that resonates with your unique circumstances. If the plan doesn't feel like it belongs to you, you're less likely to commit to it.

The first step? Shrink your financial footprint. From the budgeting principles you learned in Chapter 6, you know which expenditures are essential and which are superfluous. Historically, housing is the biggest household monthly expense. How can you reduce that? One suggestion is to pay off your mortgage sooner. And what about that car loan? Pay it off and resist the temptation of diving into another long-term commitment like a new car loan. The quicker you reduce these obligations, the faster you can boost your savings.

With a streamlined budget in place, you're better equipped for long-term planning. By adjusting your finances to reflect your actual spending patterns and needs, you'll get a clearer picture of your retirement needs.

Consider two individuals, earning $50,000 a year and with a savings goal of $500,000 for retirement. Yet, their financial landscapes can be vastly different. While you might be mortgage-free, your neighbor might grapple with a $2,200 monthly mortgage at retirement. You might have property taxes and insurance summing up to $800, while your neighbor juggles his mortgage, medical prescriptions, and supporting an adult child.

This disparity highlights the flaw in the "ten times your income" rule. It's not universally applicable. The more personalized your plan, the more likely you'll be to stick with it. It's crucial to craft a financial strategy that aligns naturally with your personal circumstances.

## Two Paths to Retirement

The first path is to take your monthly household expense number, multiply by twelve and then again by thirty, and work to pile up that cash as quickly as possible. This is the path most people envision and understandably feel overwhelmed and intimidated by.

The second path is to take control of your budget today and work to shrink your footprint. After medical expenses, housing is the largest cost for retirees. By paying off your mortgage before reaching retirement age, you can substantially decrease the monthly amount you'll need during retirement. The added advantage of a reduced monthly expenditure is that you'll require a smaller total amount to retire. A smaller monthly cost equals a smaller retirement fund, which may even allow you to retire earlier than initially planned.

You may be feeling like, "Well, I'm fifty, with twenty-eight years left on my mortgage, so I'm screwed." You are not screwed, but you have less room for error with a shorter window. Using the strategies I have laid out, you can pay off your thirty-year mortgage in less than seven years. Having a mortgage is a forced savings. Shrinking your footprint opens the doors to more opportunities for success. Remember, you are the new architect of your choices.

If these two paths feel oversimplified, they are. The gatekeepers and fee advisors overcomplicate retirement for a reason: to make their money, too. It's not complicated at all. But just because something is simple doesn't mean it is easy. This requires an incredible amount of work, discipline, and determination. With the right mindset and game plan, you can do this.

# Chapter 13

## Ten Key Tools for Achieving Financial Security

1. **Know You've Already Won**: Everything you need to achieve your wishes is already within you. If you have the mental health and the physical ability to navigate this earth and connect with others, you already have everything you need. Remove self-doubt and move forward confidently.

2. **Educate Yourself Financially:** Grasp the basics of net worth, cash flow, income statements, and balance sheets. You don't have to be a financial pro, but learn enough so no one can talk down to you about money.

3. **Find Passion in Your Profession:** Love what you do and find the joy in serving others. If you're not passionate about your current job, it might be time to consider a change.

4. **Live within Your Means:** As a fitness guru wisely said, "Eat less, move more." Similarly, spend less and earn more. It's a straightforward formula.

5. **Acquire Assets, Not Liabilities:** Pour your money into investments, properties, or businesses that appreciate over time. Dedicate your resources—time, money, and love—to avenues that promise the best returns. Don't hesitate to walk away from unsatisfying relationships or negative influences.

6. **Ask Better Questions:** Don't ask, "Why me?" This question removes you from the situation and your ability to learn and grow from it. Ask, "What can I learn from this?" The quality of your questions determines the quality of your financial life.

7. **Determine Your True Wealth:** Measure it by asking, "How long can I maintain my desired lifestyle if I stop working today?"

8. **Assess Your Weaknesses and Strengths:** Lean on your strengths and work on your weaknesses. If you are blessed, you will find a partner in life who will help you with both.

9. **Cover Your Butt:** Ensure that you're making well-protected financial decisions. Understand the importance of risk management and always carry insurance.

10. **Give Generously:** Share your smile, time, knowledge, passion, and insights. Often, the giver reaps more joy than the receiver. Give as if your very happiness hinges on it—because it might.

# Conclusion

The world would prosper more if more people had the financial security to live their passions. The world would prosper more if more poets, mentors, teachers, fathers, and mothers lived their passion. Financial security is at the root of more of us living our passions instead of just working for a living.

I dedicated the bulk of this book to addressing and dispelling the many limiting financial beliefs I have heard from my clients, students, friends, and community. I did this because limiting financial beliefs stop people from trying, hoping, dreaming, testing, and failing. These beliefs stop us dead in our tracks and derail our journey to becoming the best versions of ourselves. The versions we are intended to be.

My goal with this book is to help you strip away all the bullshit and layers that life has put on you. The same layers and filters that we subconsciously put on ourselves.

You've reached the final page of this book. Now, I'd like you to turn back to page 22 (XXII), where you noted the date and time you began reading. Go back, review what you wrote, and calculate the time that has elapsed since then. This book is concise, so I don't imagine it took you too long. However, in the hours, days, or weeks it took you to finish, I'd venture to guess that your job, home, bills, and spouse remain unchanged. While everything appears the same, I hope that everything for you has changed. With a shift in mindset, your world has transformed, and life will never be the same again.

Imagine a world where the stock market is falling, companies are shutting down, and people are losing their jobs. Have we seen this before? I've lived through several of these myself. Now, imagine the same events happening around you, except your mortgage is paid in full, and so are your car, student loans, and credit cards. The world may be shaking around you, but you are on solid ground. Even if the floor were to fall out from under you, you're equipped with a financial parachute: six years' worth of expenses in savings.

How much grace would you have with your children, family members, and coworkers if you had this level of financial security? All the day-to-day nonsense would roll right off your back. This is what I want for you. I hope that you've recognized with the tools within this book just how quickly you can get there.

I hope to meet you in person one day and witness you living your best life, which in turn liberates others to do the same. Until that day, thank you for being you.

# Acknowledgments

My first and most heartfelt thank you is dedicated to my wife, Ivelisse. You were not only an indispensable editor for this book but also provided your love, enthusiasm, and unwavering support throughout this entire process. Your sensibility continually makes me a better person, and I am profoundly grateful to be your partner in this life.

Thank you to my professional editor, Linda Alila. Linda, you helped me transform a decade's worth of ideas—jotted on the backs of receipts, napkins, and voluminous notes—into structured and actionable insights. Your enthusiasm for my work validated this wild dream of mine.

To my children, Victor, Eiva, and Eli, each of you is unique, yet you care and love with the same intensity. It is my privilege to be in your lives, and the responsibility of being your dad is one I've never taken lightly. I thank God for you and strive not to hinder your greatness but to guide you towards rooms where you can actualize your potential. The world will benefit from your happiness and productivity.

The contents of this book have been inspired by thousands. Thank you to my parents and my wonderful family. To everyone who has hopped onto my trolley and rode along for a city block, three miles, or thirty years; you have all impacted my life and my journey. I have been touched by your kindness, friendship, and trust.

To my brother and business partner Gio: this has been one hell of a ride, and I wouldn't sign up to do it again with anyone but you.

To teacher Lateefah Abdur-Rabb, you truly intimidated me. Your stern accountability was precisely what I needed, even though 13-year-old me didn't like it at the time. To this day, you have had the most profound impact on me. Every time I write, I am transported back to your English classroom. To Mr. and Mrs. Barshop your level of education and teamwork in the school as a husband-and-wife team remains an inspiration to me.

To the many clients who have entrusted me, to the middle school finance students from whom I have learned, and to my track athletes who reminded me of our unlimited potential and inspired me to keep coaching—thank you. Your lessons are invaluable.

To school faculty, former co-workers, classmates, and friends: I have learned something from every one of you. Thank you.

# Glossary

## Financial Terms You Should Know

The following is a list of financial terms that should not intimidate you.

### APR

The Annual Percentage Rate (APR) represents the yearly interest on borrowed money. While mortgages can have durations like fifteen, twenty, or thirty years, we utilize APR to equate the cost across different loan lengths.

Short-term lenders, such as those offering payday or immediate cash loans, might reveal their interest rates but often keep the actual APR under wraps. Consider a loan promoting an 11% interest rate due in a week. This isn't the same as another loan with an 11% annual rate. To deduce the APR for such a loan, one would multiply this rate by the fifty-two weeks in a year, resulting in an alarming 572% APR.

Such towering rates render short-term loans exceptionally dangerous. Borrowing a mere $600 could lead to over $3,400 in interest, assuming no compounding. With compounding and potential missed payments, breaking free from this debt might seem nearly impossible.

## Assets

Assets grow in value and, most often, put money in your pockets. Examples of assets are collectibles, businesses, real estate (you rent to others), intellectual property such as music, content, technology you created, or something you have written.

## Bonds

Think of a bond as an IOU or a promise to repay you. Bonds can be issued by corporations such as Apple and Microsoft, municipalities such as your local township, or the Treasury. In each instance, the bond issuer is trying to raise money for a purpose. You, as the investor, would lend money to the bond issuer, and they, in turn, would promise to pay you back all of your money, plus interest. This makes you a lender to the company, your township, or the Treasury.

## Budget

A budget is a plan you make for how you will manage and spend your money. You could make a budget for your next vacation, your night out with friends, or a budget your household this month.

A budget is an essential part of being successful with money.

## Cash Flow

If you are running a business, your cash flow is the amount of money you have at your disposal every month after your expenses. If you manage your household, your cash flow is the money you have left over after all your expenses.

You can and should measure your monthly cash flow. Knowing your cash flow will help you in your daily decision-making process. You can plan and anticipate to reach your desired cash flow. If you are not measuring your cash flow, you are not planning but reacting.

## Commodities

A commodity is a tangible good that can be purchased, sold, or used in trade for another commodity. Examples are corn, wheat, sugar, and gold.

## ETF Exchange Traded Funds

Much like index funds, ETFs are passively managed, providing great diversification and low costs. Unlike an index fund, ETFs are more liquid, allowing you to buy and sell during market hours, and there are no account minimums. ETFs are much more beginner-friendly.

The S&P 500 ETFs and index funds target the five hundred largest companies in the United States. These funds offer exposure to some of the most successful and stable companies. Examples include Vanguard S&P 500 ETF (VOO) and SPDR S&P 500 ETF Trust (SPY).

## Index Funds

Index funds are a basket of all the stocks within a specific index. Index funds offer you the ability to spread your exposure for fewer fees than mutual funds.

## Interest Rates: Compound, Simple, Variable

Grasping the nuances of interest rates is crucial, not just for borrowing but also for investing. When you invest with simple interest, a 4% annual percentage rate (APR) on a $10,000 investment will yield $400 at the end of the first year. In the subsequent years, you'd consistently earn the same $400 annually. However, compound interest paints a different picture. Under identical terms (4% APR on a $10,000 investment), the first year still brings in $400. But the second year calculates the 4% APR on your increased balance of $10,400, resulting in $416. This pattern continues, with each year's interest compounding on the progressively growing balance. When you're on the borrowing side, whether for a car, home, business, or short-term loan, you're typically presented with an APR. This rate is pivotal in determining your actual borrowing cost.

A brief note about adjustable-rate mortgages or ARM: initially, an ARM might seem more attractive due to its typically lower rates than the prevailing market rate. But there's a catch. These rates adjust according to the prime rate, which the Federal Reserve determines. If the Fed aims to stimulate borrowing and spending, they'll drop the prime rate. Conversely, if they're curtailing inflation and trying to suppress a rising price of goods, they'll raise the prime rate. Consequently, a loan that began at a 4% interest rate might swiftly escalate to 12%.

Different interest rates come with their intricacies, but the key lies in knowing how to calculate the true borrowing cost.

## Liabilities

Liabilities decrease in value and take money out of your pocket. Examples of liabilities are toys, ATV's motorcycles, cars, and more. It is a liability if the item is worth less than what you paid for at the time of resale. Many people believe their home is their largest asset, but a home you live in is a liability because it takes money out of your pocket. Even though the home appreciates in value, you must pay for the loan and the interest. However, if you own the same home but someone else lives in it and pays rent to you (in essence, paying the loan), that property is converted from a liability to an asset.

## Mutual Funds

Mutual funds are a basket of stocks, bonds, or both. They are professionally managed and come with management fees. Utilizing a basket approach allows you to invest in similar companies without exposing yourself to just one company.

## Opportunity Cost

Opportunity cost involves evaluating the potential value of forgone choices. Consider this: In 2001, Apple unveiled its first iPod with a $400 price tag. Instead of buying that iPod, imagine investing in Apple stock. Back then, shares hovered under $1, allowing for the purchase of roughly four hundred shares with that $400. With subsequent stock splits in 2005, 2014, and 2020, and assuming you held on to those shares, their current value at $180 per share would exceed $4 million.

## Overdraft

Overdraft is when you spend more from your checking account than you have.

Some banks will enroll you into overdraft protection without your asking. This may appear as a feature or a perk, but it is not. Overdraft protection allows you to draw more from your bank account than you have. It brings along heavy overdraft fees with every transaction that pulls you under. This is a huge revenue generator for banks, and it doesn't help the consumer build responsible spending habits.

## Prime Rate

In the U.S., the prime rate is the floor for borrowing rates. Financial institutions base their offers on this rate when lending. However, it's a misconception to assume borrowers can access this foundational rate on their loans. In practice, lenders invariably add a premium to the prime rate before extending their loan rates to consumers.

## Repossession

Repossession is to reclaim ownership of personal property linked or attached to a loan. Most commonly, vehicles are repossessed when a borrower fails to pay on the car loan as agreed upon in the purchase contract.

Lenders have greater confidence in their likelihood of being repaid by the borrower if they can secure a loan with personal property. Auto loans and some personal loans are secured or collateralized by a car. The lender can repossess that car if the borrower defaults on their payments.

## Stocks, Shares, and Equities

A stock is a fractional ownership of a company. When you own a stock, you won't own all of the available stock, which means you share ownership of the company. Stocks are also called shares. The shares themselves have value and can also be referred to as equities. Ultimately, they all point to the same fractional ownership unit.

## Ten-Year Treasury Notes (T-Notes)

A ten-year T-Note is a bond issued by our Treasury. Treasury bonds are considered the safest investment in the U.S. because our government does not default on our debts despite the dysfunction in our government.

## Yields

The yields is the profitability generated by your investment.

# Appendix

---

# Financial Relationships You Should Understand

## Money Makes Money

It took me a long time to realize that money isn't primarily for buying things or paying off debt; it's for making more money. Of course, we use money for purchases and to settle debts, but these are not its primary functions. When you grasp this concept, your money becomes far more efficient. You work to earn money, live modestly, and accumulate funds to invest for your benefit, creating more money.

Big institutional money moves with the sole intent of generating more wealth. If there is profit to be made in the stock market, money will flow into it, which is evident when stock prices rise.

When big money sees better or higher returns possible elsewhere, such as in the real estate market, it shifts away from the stock market (causing stock prices to drop) and moves into real estate, leading to an increase in property prices. Conversely, when these institutions believe better returns can be found in undervalued stocks, they pull out of real estate (potentially crashing the housing market) and reinvest in the stock market where higher returns are anticipated.

This is a cycle. The big or "smart" institutional money moves toward better investment returns before the trend begins. When the average investor notices this trend, the best gains have often already been realized by institutional investors.

You might think this puts you at a disadvantage. However, you're not doomed. Suppose we understand that money flows from one market to another, impacting prices. In that case, we can strategically invest in real estate when stocks are hot and shift our focus to stocks when their prices fall because big money is migrating to real estate.

Understanding these dynamics helps us manage the emotions that arise when we see an asset class plummet or skyrocket. Our instinct might be to jump on the rocket before it leaves or to abandon the sinking ship before it hits the bottom. While these reactions are natural and logical, they are not beneficial for investing. These shifts in markets are called corrections and they happen in cycles. On average, we have a stock market correction every eight to ten years. Fear of unrecoverable losses urges many to move on impulse, but understanding your ability to wait out the current market correction will be key to your success.

## Ten-Year T-Notes, the Market, and the Consumer

If you listen to or watch any financial news, you'll frequently hear about the yield of the ten-year Treasury note (T-note). The yield represents the money the bond will generate over a decade.

When the yield is rising, it indicates that the Treasury is offering higher returns to attract investors back to T-notes. This increase typically occurs when the Treasury needs to entice investors away from higher-risk assets, such as stocks.

Conversely, if investors are not investing in T-notes, it often means they are channeling their funds into riskier assets like stocks. As more money flows into the stock market, stock prices ("seedlings") will likely rise. This underscores the relationship between the yield on ten-year T-notes and market behavior. A falling yield suggests that T-notes, which are low-risk investments, are in demand. This demand usually increases when investors move away from stocks due to fear or uncertainty about the market.

## Supply and Demand

The availability of a sandwich or semiconductor chip will have the greatest impact on its demand and ultimately the price the market will give it. Even if a product is not amazing, it could be valued highly because it is in low supply. Something could be phenomenal, but if there is a ridiculous and abundant supply, its perceived value would decline.

During the pandemic, we saw the price of toilet paper hit unbelievable price levels because of high demand. The paper wasn't suddenly magical in its properties, it just wasn't as readily available. Driven by the fear of scarcity, consumers bought more paper more often, which depleted grocery store shelves. This surge in demand motivated others to believe there would be a shortage, which compelled many to buy in large quantities as well, adding to the demand.

Demand is not efficient, nor is it always attributable to great quality; it is often a result of consumer psychology and emotion.

Increased demand for ten-year T-Notes means the yield will go down. If you hear on the radio that the yield on the T-Note is down, it's a signal that investors are concerned and are seeking security.

## Insurance: A Shield against Risk

Insurance acts as a safeguard, transferring significant financial risks from your shoulders to the insurance company. It's vital for high-value assets like your home, car, or even your potential earnings if become disabled or pass away prematurely.

Consider this: if you're in a car accident, the last thing you'd want is to dig deep into your savings to replace your vehicle. Or imagine your home succumbs to a fire. You wouldn't want to deplete your savings covering hotel stays, reconstruction, and the replacement of lost belongings. And, while no amount can truly compensate for the loss of a loved one, should you pass away, you'd want to ensure that your family isn't burdened financially in your absence.

A policy covering losses up to hundreds of thousands is vital for financial planning. You aim to establish financial security, build a savings and investment portfolio, and not risk losing it all due to one catastrophic event. Insurance protection is logical for significant life assets. However, it's not sensible for small, easily replaceable items. Decline offers in your online shopping cart to add insurance to your electronic purchase or suggestions at the checkout counter of big box stores. Your money is better spent working for you rather than benefiting the retailer.

## The Federal Reserve: Raising Rates vs. Lowering Rates

The role of the Federal Reserve system in our economy is to maintain unemployment at around 3% and inflation near 3%. The Fed manipulates the markets using two primary levers. The first is by adjusting interest rates. The second lever involves injecting or withdrawing money into the banking system. This is often referred to as "printing" money, a term frequently mentioned in the news.

Raising interest rates makes borrowing more expensive and restrictive for businesses, potential homebuyers, investors, and speculators. Increasing rates is akin to pouring cold water on a hot market. Conversely, lowering interest rates makes borrowing more accessible for these groups, fostering overall market growth. Decreasing rates is like adding coal and oxygen to a slow-burning fire.

Sometimes, simply lowering rates isn't enough to encourage banks to lend more to businesses and consumers. In such cases, the Fed buys bonds from the banks, loading them with super-cheap capital. With this influx of funds, banks logically put it to work by lending it to consumers through mortgages, car loans, and personal loans.

Conversely, when raising rates doesn't cool the market quickly enough, and inflation begins to reach significantly uncomfortable levels or unsustainable peaks for average Americans, the Fed retracts the money it has lent to the banks. This action causes banks to slow down on lending approvals, sometimes almost to a halt.

Adjusting interest rates and controlling the flow of money impacts Main Street and everyday Americans, underscoring the importance of understanding how the Federal Reserve uses these levers to influence unemployment and inflation.

# Bibliography

Tolle, Eckhart. *A New Earth* (New York: Penguin Books, 2005).

[2] Tolle, Eckhart. *A New Earth* (New York: Penguin Books, 2005).

[3] Tolle, Eckhart. *The Power of Now: A Guide to Spiritual Enlightenment* (London, England: Hodder Paperback, 2001).

[4] "Despite Financial Stress, many Americans are too worried about job stability to take PTO" https://www.bankrate.com/credit-cards/news/pto-and-financial-stress/.

[5] "How Americans View Their Jobs" https://www.pewresearch.org/social-trends/2023/03/30/how-americans-view-their-jobs/.

[6] "How the American Middle Class Has Changed in the Past Five Decades," Pew Research Center, last modified April 20, 2022, https://www.pewresearch.org/short-reads/2022/04/20/how-the-american-middle-class-has-changed-in-the-past-five-decades/.

[7] Sam Carr, "How Many Ads Do We See a Day in 2024?" Lunio, https://lunio.ai/blog/strategy/how-many-ads-do-we-see-a-day/.

[8] Clear, James. *Atomic Habits: An Easy & Proven Way to Build Good Habits & Break Bad Ones* (New York: Avery, an imprint of Penguin Random House, 2018).

[9] "Credit Card Statistics: Debt, Balances, Fees and More [2024]" https://www.themoneymanual.com/credit-card-statistics/.

[10] "2024 Credit Card Debt Statistics" https://www.lendingtree.com/credit-cards/credit-card-debt-statistics/.

[11] "Poll: 60% who have credit card debt have owed their creditors for at least 12 months" https://www.creditcards.com/statistics/credit-card-debt-poll/.

[12] "What is the highest credit card interest rate?" https://wallethub.com/answers/cc/highest-credit-card-interest-rate-2140660307/.

[13] https://www.federalreserve.gov/publications/2023-economic-well-being-of-us-households-in-2022-expenses.htm.

[14] "Percentage Distribution of Household Income in the United States in 2022." Statista, May 22, 2024, https://www.statista.com/statistics/203183/percentage-distribution-of-household-income-in-the-us/.

[15] "Credit Card Debt: 1 in 4 Americans Fall Deeper Into Debt Each Month (2023 Data)" https://listwithclever.com/research/average-american-credit-card-debt-**2023/.**

# Author Biography

Edward Sanchez is a seasoned financial consultant with over two decades of experience in bankruptcy and finance. Since 1999, he has dedicated his career to financial consulting, specializing in credit counseling. He is the co-founder and president of a nationwide credit counseling firm that has significantly impacted the financial literacy of over 440,000 students.

Edward has also been committed to educating the next generation, teaching financial literacy to junior high students for 12 years. His passion for youth development extends to the athletic field, where he has coached a track and field team for grades 4th through 8th alongside his wife for the same duration.

Edward's academic background includes graduating from Lane Tech High School in Chicago and earning a bachelor's degree from the University of Illinois at Urbana-Champaign. Beyond his professional life, Edward is a husband and father of three. He is an avid reader and woodworker and enjoys running. Though a native of Chicago, he now resides just outside the city with his wife and children.